Canada

Canada

BY BARBARA RADCLIFFE ROGERS
AND STILLMAN D. ROGERS

Enchantment of the World
Second Series

Children's Press®

A Division of Grolier Publishing

NEW YORK   LONDON   HONG KONG   SYDNEY
DANBURY, CONNECTICUT

Frontispiece: An Inuit snow sculpture in front of the Winter Snow Palace at Quebec's winter carnival

Consultant: Anthony B. Chan, Ph.D., Director, Canadian Studies Center, and Chair, B.A. program in Canadian Studies, University of Washington; Principal Investigator of the National Resource Center for the Study of Canada supported by the Department of Education, Washington, D.C.

Please note: All statistics are as up-to-date as possible at the time of publication.

Visit Children's Press on the Internet: http://publishing.grolier.com

Book Production by Herman Adler Design Group

Library of Congress Cataloging-in-Publication Data

Rogers, Barbara Radcliffe.
 Canada / by Barbara Radcliffe Rogers and Stillman D. Rogers.
  p. cm. — (Enchantment of the world. Second series)
 Includes bibliographical references and index.
 Summary: Introduces our northern neighbor, its history, geography, government, economy, plants and animals, people, and culture.
 ISBN 0-516-21076-9
 1. Canada Juvenile literature. [1. Canada.] I. Rogers, Stillman, 1939– . II. Title. III. Series.
F1008.2.R56 2000
971—dc21   99-37400
                       CIP

GROLIER PUBLISHING

Canada

Cover photo: The Parliament building and Rideau Canal in Ottawa

Contents

Quebec City and the Saint Lawrence River

An Inuit carving

A Country of Contrasts

8

An Inuit village on Baffin Island in the new territory of Nunavut

Opposite: **Quebec City in the province of Quebec**

Canada is the second-largest country in the world, covering more than two-fifths of the continent of North America. Although it is larger than the United States, only one-tenth as many people live in Canada. A little more than 31 million people live in this vast country, mainly along its two coasts and in a narrow band along its southern border, where most of its cities lie.

With so much land stretching from the Atlantic to the Pacific Oceans, it is not surprising that Canada is a country of great contrasts. The deeply cut fjords of Newfoundland's coast are not at all like the rolling prairies of Saskatchewan, and the lives of the French-speaking people in the sophisticated city of Montreal, Quebec, are quite different from the lives of the Inuits in the new territory of Nunavut.

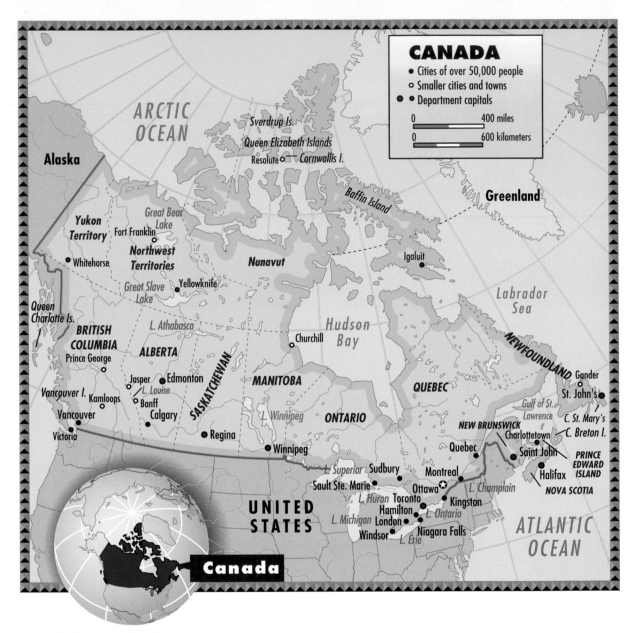

CANADA

- ● Cities of over 50,000 people
- ○ Smaller cities and towns
- ● Department capitals

0   400 miles
0   600 kilometers

ARCTIC OCEAN

Alaska

Sverdrup Is.
Queen Elizabeth Islands
Resolute ○ ● Cornwallis I.

Baffin Island

Greenland

Yukon Territory
Fort Franklin
Great Bear Lake
Northwest Territories
Whitehorse
Great Slave Lake
Yellowknife

Nunavut

Igaluit

Labrador Sea

Queen Charlotte Is.

L. Athabasca

Churchill

Hudson Bay

NEWFOUNDLAND

BRITISH COLUMBIA
Prince George
ALBERTA
SASKATCHEWAN
MANITOBA
Jasper
L. Louise
Edmonton
Vancouver I.
Kamloops
Banff
Calgary
Vancouver
Victoria
Regina
L. Winnipeg
ONTARIO
Winnipeg

QUEBEC

Gander
St. John's
Gulf of St. Lawrence
C. St. Mary's
C. Breton I.
NEW BRUNSWICK
Charlottetown
Quebec
Saint John
PRINCE EDWARD ISLAND
Halifax
NOVA SCOTIA

UNITED STATES

L. Superior
Sault Ste. Marie
Sudbury
Montreal
Ottawa ✪
L. Champlain
L. Huron
Toronto
Kingston
Hamilton
L. Ontario
London
L. Michigan
Niagara Falls
Windsor
L. Erie

ATLANTIC OCEAN

Canada

Geopolitical map of Canada

Between the fishing villages on the rocky Atlantic shores and the forested mountainsides of the Pacific Coast, the people are as different as the lands they live in. Ancestors of many people in

A fishing community in Newfoundland

Touring the streets of Quebec City by horse-drawn carriage

the Atlantic provinces came from Scotland and Ireland. In the neighboring province of Quebec, French is the official language, while the cities of Toronto and Vancouver have Chinatown neighborhoods that are large enough to be cities on their own.

Canada is an exciting place to be. Its cities are lively and modern, decorated with bright flowers and filled with interesting things to do. In old Quebec, you can ride a horse-drawn carriage through streets that look just like those in Europe. Or you can ride a dogsled right in the middle of the city during Quebec's winter carnival. If you go west to Calgary, you can put on a cowboy hat and join in the Calgary Stampede—the Wild West, Canadian style.

Although Canada may often resemble the United States, it is really a very different country, with its own history, geography, and way of life. But it would be a mistake to think that all Canadians— or all of Canada—are alike. Its many contrasts are what make it so interesting.

Fish, Forests, Farms, and Frost

CANADA SHARES THE WHOLE OF THE TOP OF THE NORTH American continent with the U.S. state of Alaska, from the U.S. border almost to the North Pole. The magnetic north pole is actually inside Canada, 200 miles (322 kilometers) north of Resolute on Cornwallis Island, part of the new territory of Nunavut.

Even though the land stretches thousands of miles to the north, most Canadians live within 200 miles (322 km) of the U.S. border, along a thin corridor of fertile farmland and prairie. North of that narrow band stretch hundreds of miles of wilderness forests, lakes, ponds, and rivers. The people who live here are called "First Nations Peoples" in Canada. They are the descendants of Canada's original people—the Inuits and other groups. Farther north, it is too cold for trees to grow, and the land is permanently frozen, covered with ice and snow.

Opposite: **Moraine Lake and the Rocky Mountains in Banff National Park, Alberta**

Some land in northern Canada is permanently covered with ice and snow. Here, a snowmobile pulls a sled on Baffin Island.

The Continents Collide

To understand Canada's land, it helps to know something about tectonic plates. Scientists believe the Earth has an outer shell made up of about 30 pieces called tectonic plates. These plates have been moving very slowly for hundreds of millions of years. Billions of years ago, all the continents were part of one huge landmass called Pangaea. Over time, pressure from inside the Earth—due to the movement of the plates—caused this supercontinent to break up. Its pieces began to move away from one another. Sometimes the edge of one plate slid under the edge of another plate, making them fold and bend. This folding and bending created the mountains we see today.

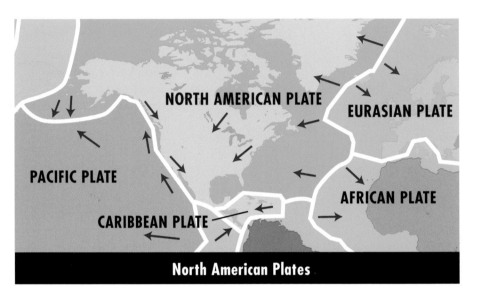

North American Plates

The Great Canadian Shield

The Canadian Shield, which covers about half of Canada, is part of that original continent. It is made up of ancient rock, called Precambrian rock. More than 570 million years old, it is among the oldest exposed rock on Earth. The Canadian Shield includes all the land north of the Saint Lawrence River

and Lake Superior and runs in a huge arc from Lake Superior northwest almost to the Alaskan border. Nearly all of Canada's Arctic lands are also part of the Canadian Shield.

Newfoundland tundra in autumn

Much of the soil in this region is poor, because its topsoil was scraped off during the last ice ages, when sheets of ice more than 2 miles (3 km) thick covered the soil. Today, it is a land of rivers and lakes, with huge forests of spruce and fir trees in the south. In the north, the trees give way to tundra— land where only mosses, lichens, and scrubby low bushes can grow—and finally to ice and snow in the Arctic. In the middle of the Canadian Shield, on the north, is one of the world's largest bays, Hudson Bay, named for the explorer Henry Hudson, who also discovered the Hudson River in New York.

East of the Canadian Shield lie the Atlantic provinces of New Brunswick, Nova Scotia, Prince Edward Island, and Newfoundland/Labrador. This rocky and mountainous land is the eastern cordillera, a chain of mountains pushed up out of the Earth's crust millions of years ago as the plates collided.

The mountains that start in Newfoundland and continue into Nova Scotia and New Brunswick are part of the Appalachian Range. Before the supercontinent of Pangaea broke apart, they were part of the same range as the mountains of Scotland.

The island of Newfoundland is combined with the large mainland area of Labrador into one province. At their closest point they are only 10 miles (16 km) apart, across the Strait of Belle Isle. Labrador borders the province of Quebec, but most of its communication with the outside world is by sea, through Newfoundland.

Prince Edward Island, often called PEI, is the smallest province. It lies off the north shore of Nova Scotia, which is almost an island itself, attached to New Brunswick by only

One Island, Three Plates

Canada's small island province of Newfoundland was formed by parts of three of the Earth's tectonic plates. On the west side is the edge of the original North American Plate. Next to it, forming the center of the island, is land that was pushed up from the bottom of the sea that once separated the continents. On the east side is rock that was pulled from the Eurasian Plate and the African Plate when North America drifted west again.

When the continents split apart, a hole was torn in the Earth's crust, and some of the Earth's mantle—or sublayer—was pushed up into the hole. This very rare landform can be seen in Newfoundland's Gros Morne National Park. Plants will not grow on the mantle.

a 17-mile (27-km)-wide strip of land. PEI, which until recently could be reached only by ferry, is now linked to the rest of Canada via the new Confederation Bridge.

A farm on Prince Edward Island, Canada's smallest province

Central Canada

More than half the citizens of Canada live in the provinces of Ontario and Quebec, the major industrial and manufacturing

Quebec City is on the Saint Lawrence River.

areas. These provinces produce more than three-fourths of all Canada's manufactured products. Four of the five Great Lakes—Superior, Huron, Erie, and Ontario—along with the Saint Lawrence River, form the border between the United States and central Canada. The fifth—Lake Michigan—lies entirely within the United States. Goods are shipped to markets all over the world through these waterways.

This part of the Canadian Shield is rich in minerals and covered with forests that provide pulp for Canada's paper industry. To the north, river systems generate electric power for Canada and the northeastern United States. Quebec is Canada's main producer of pulp and paper, as well as electricity.

The Prairie Provinces

The Central Plains, a great area of fertile, mostly rolling lands, lie west of the Canadian Shield. Once part of the ocean bottom, this region was thrust up as the North American Plate moved west and collided with the plate that lay under the Pacific Ocean. Canada's great plains are connected to the plains of the central United States. This area is Canada's "grain belt" and important to the agriculture of the country. The plains stretch west to the foothills of the northern Rocky Mountains, covering a small part of Manitoba and most of the provinces of Saskatchewan and Alberta.

A large part of central Manitoba is filled with water. The largest body of water is Lake Winnipeg, and three smaller lakes to its west combine to cover an area almost as big as Lake Winnipeg.

The plains in Saskatchewan

A Dinosaur Supermarket

When the floor of the ancient ocean was thrust upward, it became a tropical land of mountains and volcanoes, inhabited by prehistoric creatures. Today, Saskatchewan has some of the continent's finest fossil deposits, which tell scientists something about life before humans walked on Earth. A nearly complete *Tyrannosaurus rex* skeleton was found near Eastend, and the fossil remains of an enormous crocodile-like creature named "Big Bert" were found along the Carrot River. Visitors there can get a close-up look at the work of paleontologists as they dig in what they laughingly call their "supermarket of dinosaur bones."

Canada's three territories—Yukon, Northwest Territories, and Nunavut—cover the huge area north of the prairie provinces with lowlands, lakes, bays, and islands that stretch to the North Pole. Frozen much of the year, this flat area is covered in tundra and taiga. Only low plants, mosses, lichens, shrubs, and stunted trees grow on the tundra, while the taiga has forests of spruce, pine, and fir trees that can survive severe winters.

Taiga in the Yukon is covered with thick forests.

The West

When the North American Plate crunched into the Pacific Plate, the collision forced its western edge over part of the Pacific Plate. The edge of the North American Plate pushed up and buckled, like a car fender in an accident, creating the Canadian Rocky Mountains and the Coast Mountains along the Pacific Ocean. These mountains are younger than the mountains in eastern North America and have not been ground down by huge glaciers. As a result, they are taller and more jagged.

The Rocky Mountains are taller and more jagged than the Appalachian Mountains in the east.

Canada's Geographical Features

Highest Elevation: Mount Logan, 19,524 feet (5,951 m), in the Yukon Territory

Longest River: The Mackenzie River (1,120 miles [1,802 km]), in Northwest Territories, which ranks twelfth in the world

Largest Lake Entirely within Canada: Great Bear Lake, 12,275 square miles (31,792 sq km)

Largest Island: Baffin Island, 183,810 square miles (476,068 sq km), the fifth-largest island in the world

Highest Average Temperature: 70°F (21°C) in July in Ottawa, Ontario

Lowest Average Temperature: −26°F (−33°C) in February, in Arctic Bay, Northwest Territories

Longest Bridge: Pierre Laporte in Quebec, 291 feet (89 m)

Largest Dam: Syncrude Tailings, the largest dam in the world

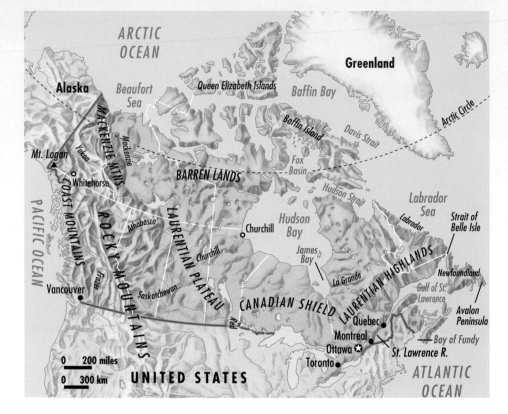

This plate collision is still going on. As the Pacific Plate pushes under the North American Plate, it melts from the heat inside the Earth. In places where this occurs, there is always the chance of volcanoes erupting.

The western cordillera is a beautiful and mountainous place with vast forests and wilderness. The provinces of British

Columbia and the Yukon Territory are in this area. The Pacific coast is rough and craggy with many inlets and small bays. Many small islands lie offshore, including the huge Vancouver Island and a group of large islands called the Queen Charlotte Islands.

Very close to the ocean, the tall Coast Mountains form a solid wall, the first barrier to the interior. Beyond them is a plateau—an area of flat, high land—and then more mountains push up, first smaller mountains and then the high Rockies. The Rocky Mountains, together with the Coast Mountains, form a barrier against storms and winds that travel east from the Pacific Ocean. As a result, most of the moisture carried in the winds falls on the coast and in the mountains as rain and snow. Very little of it crosses over to irrigate the central plains.

From Warm to Very Cold

The part of Canada that borders the United States is on the northern edge of the temperate zone—the part of the world where temperatures are neither very hot nor very cold. Just a few miles north of the border, however, the temperatures drop. Summers are short, and the growing season for trees and

The frozen tundra in Manitoba

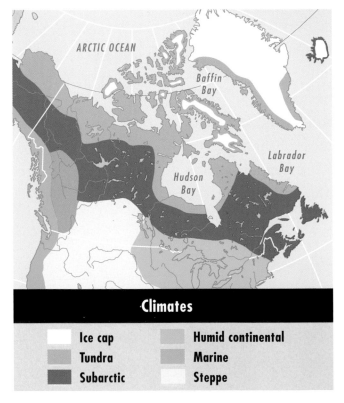

ARCTIC OCEAN

Baffin Bay

Labrador Bay

Hudson Bay

Climates

- Ice cap
- Tundra
- Subarctic
- Humid continental
- Marine
- Steppe

plants barely allows them time to get bigger from year to year. In the far north lies the Arctic zone, where almost nothing grows. While low brush and lichens can be found in some places they are covered with snow and ice most of the year.

The eastern provinces extend way out into the Atlantic Ocean, which gives them a natural heating and cooling system. The Gulf Stream, a current of warm water that flows north from the Caribbean Sea along the east coast of North America, comes close to shore here. This current of water carries an air current above it that

Looking at Canada's Cities

Toronto, the capital of Ontario, was founded in 1793. The city, with its surrounding metropolitan area, is home to 4,263,757 people. The average daily temperature ranges from 54° to 73°F (12° to 23°C) in June, and from 16° to 30°F (−9° to −1°C) in January. Famous landmarks include the CN (Canadian National) Tower, Toronto City Hall, Royal Ontario Museum, and the shore of Lake Ontario. At 1,815 feet (553 meters), the CN Tower is the world's tallest free-standing structure.

Montreal, with a population of 3,326,510, is a major eastern seaport. It was founded in 1642. The average daily temperature is 62°F (16°C) in June and 10°F (−12°C) in January. Mount Royal and the Saint Joseph Oratory, Saint Helen's Island, Old Montreal, the Olympic Tower, Atwater Market, and the Locks of the Saint Lawrence Seaway are all outstanding sights in the city.

Vancouver, British Columbia, is on Canada's west coast. It was founded in 1885. Its population is 1,831,665. The average daily temperature ranges from 52° to 69°F (11° to 21°C) in June, and from 32° to 41°F (0° to 5°C) in January. Well known landmarks include the Canadian Pavilion from Expo '86, Stanley Park, Chinatown, Capilano Suspension Bridge, and the Coast Mountains, which rise directly behind the city.

---

regulates temperatures along the east coast like a giant thermostat. It warms the area in winter and cools it in summer.

In January, daytime temperatures in Nova Scotia and Newfoundland are about 30°Fahrenheit (−1°Celsius). July and August temperatures are in the high sixties to mid seventies Fahrenheit (low to mid twenties Celsius) because of the cooling effect of the ocean. These warmer temperatures make the growing season longer, and many food crops are grown from April through October. The annual rainfall of 54 to 57 inches (137 to 145 centimeters) in these coastal provinces keeps crops well watered all year too.

The area along the U.S. border, away from these moderating ocean currents, has longer, colder winters. Winter in Quebec and Toronto may last five to six months, with January temperatures about 10°F (6°C) colder than in the ocean-

Fish, Forests, Farms, and Frost **25**

Many people enjoy ice skating on Rideau Canal in Ottawa.

facing cities. Quebec, Montreal, and Ottawa have ice-skating rinks that are frozen solid all winter long in their many parks. In summer, their temperatures average about 7°F (4°C) warmer than in Nova Scotia. The growing season is about the same as Nova Scotia's, but the ground may freeze several inches deep in the winter.

Midwinter is colder on the Central Plains because of the frigid winds that come down from the Arctic. January daytime temperatures in Alberta average 5°F (–15°C) and get as low as 0°F(–18°C) in Saskatchewan and Manitoba. Because the Rocky Mountains catch most of the moisture blowing from the Pacific Ocean, rainfall here is very low, averaging 0.5 to less than 3 inches (1.3 to 7.6 cm) a month.

As in the Atlantic Provinces, the ocean effect of the Pacific keeps west coast winters warmer, with average daily January temperatures in Vancouver of 36°F (2°C). In summer, ocean breezes keep the temperatures during the day at 60° to 67°F (16°–19°C), about the same as Halifax, in Nova Scotia.

Rainfall along the coast is heavy—from 2.5 to more than 8.5 inches (6.4 to 21.6 cm) per month between October and June for a total of 58 inches (147 cm) annually. Inland at Prince George however, the mountain effect limits rainfall to less than 1 inch (2.5 cm) in April and about 2 inches (5 cm) the rest of the year.

Yukon, the Northwest Territories, and Nunavut share the tundra and frozen lands of the northern and Arctic regions. Average daytime temperature in the winter is as low as −14°F (−26°C). Temperatures rise above freezing in the northern areas only during June, July, and August and in the southern part of the Northwest Territories from May to October, when they reach 64° to 71°F (18° to 22°C). Rainfall here is seldom more than 1 inch (2.5 cm) a month in the far north or 2.5 inches (6.4 cm) in some southern parts during summer and fall, so the territories have little or no agriculture.

Dancing Lights

In the Northwest Territories and Nunavut, and sometimes in the northern areas of other provinces, the winter sky is lit at night by the aurora borealis (northern lights). Great sheets of light—usually white or blue but often other colors—sweep across the dark sky. Sometimes these lights look like curtains billowing in the wind, and other times they appear as dancing beams and bands of light. The northern lights are caused by solar particles hitting Earth's atmosphere.

Canada's Wildlife

Colorful maple leaves during the fall

WITH SO MUCH WILD AND UNINHABITED LAND, IT seems fitting that Canada should have chosen the beaver and the maple leaf as its national symbols. These symbols represent Canada's wilderness, where plants and animals thrive undisturbed by humans. The beaver's silhouette is also the symbol of Canada's national park system, which preserves the nation's natural treasures, its wild landmarks and habitats.

Canada's tremendous variety of landscapes, the plants and trees that grow there, and its plentiful wildlife are best seen through a "tour" of some of its many national parks. The parks of each region serve as showcases of its environment—land set aside by the government to protect wildlife and ecosystems and for people to enjoy. Often, other protected reserves that are home to more native animals, birds, sea life, or plants are near the parks.

Opposite: **Wildlife is protected in Alberta's Jasper National Park.**

The steep-walled fjords at Newfoundland's Gros Morne National Park look like pictures of Norway. In Gros Morne, the mountains are suddenly interrupted by the sea or by land-locked lakes at the foot of cliffs that are 1/2 mile (1 km) tall. The park has been named a UNESCO World Heritage Site because of a unique mountain called Tablelands. The mountain's bare reddish landscape of crumbling rock is a section

This frozen fjord is in Labrador, Newfoundland.

Who Says Rodents Aren't Cute?

The beaver, a large rodent that inhabits the vast regions of central Canada, is best known for its unique ability to fell trees by chewing right through them, and for its skill in building dams. Beavers have been called the world's first engineers. But it was their valuable fur pelts that attracted the early settlers and trappers. The beaver has been used as a symbol in Canada since the 1600s and is shown on the five-cent coin.

of Earth's mantle. The Earth's mantle usually lies 1 mile (1.6 km) or more underground. It was forced to the surface here 450 million years ago as the Earth's plates moved closer together. Geologists come from all over the world to study this rare exposure of the mantle. Black bears live in the park, along with the many moose that feed in its low peat bogs.

Terra Nova, a smaller park in Newfoundland, protects a stretch of the coastline where fishing families once lived in isolated towns called outports. Its gentle shore, wooded hills, and lakes are home to moose, bears, and smaller animals, all

A Plant That Eats Bugs

The pitcher plant is the provincial flower of Newfoundland, and its bright-red bulblike blossoms decorate the island's many low bogs. The wet, acid soil of the bogs has few nutrients, so the pitcher plant has another source of food. Insects are attracted to its red flowers and the edges of its large pitcher-shaped leaves, but they cannot cling to the slippery inside surface. Soon they fall into the pitcher, where they drown in the rainwater that has collected there. The pitcher plant then absorbs the nutrients from the water. Newfoundlanders just wish these plants would eat more mosquitoes.

of which are often seen by the many visitors who camp, hike, and boat in the park. Herds of caribou live on the rocky flat land east and west of the park, including the huge Avalon herd of 13,000 animals. Travelers on the southern coast of the Avalon Peninsula often see caribou munching mosses at the roadside. This is the farthest south a herd of this size can be found anywhere in the world.

Although moose are seen nearly everywhere in Newfoundland, they are not native to the island. The entire moose population (of about 125,000 animals) is descended from six moose brought from other provinces in 1878 and 1904.

Very few places in the world have as many seabird nesting sites as Newfoundland. More than 5.5 million breeding pairs live in a dozen major colonies. Baccalieu Island alone is home to 3 million nesting pairs of Leach's storm-petrels. North America's largest population of puffins nest on an island near St. John's, the capital city.

Puffins are seabirds with colorful bills.

The world's highest tides flow in and out of the Bay of Fundy between Nova Scotia and New Brunswick. They reach 48 feet (nearly 15 m), the height of a four-story building, each day. These tides have cut away mountainsides to form towering cliffs and caves and are so powerful that they force the wide St. John River to reverse direction. Near Fundy National Park, giant sea stacks, tall oddly shaped rock towers, stand offshore where they were stranded as the land around them was worn away.

Huge rocks on the Bay of Fundy, New Brunswick

The Little World of a Big Iceberg

The waters north of Newfoundland are often called "Iceberg Alley" because so many icebergs drift past in the spring and summer. These icebergs are "calved" (dropped) from glaciers on Baffin Island and the Danish island of Greenland.

Icebergs create a wildlife ecosystem as they float along, attracting seabirds, fish, and whales that feed on the plankton that thrives in the water around icebergs. Kittywakes and other seabirds hitch rides on top of the icebergs.

Because of the churning tides, the Bay of Fundy and its rivers and tidal marshes are filled with nutrients that provide food for sea and bird life. During the August migrations, hundreds of thousands of birds stop at Mary's Point to feast in these rich waters. More varieties of whales are seen more often off the Fundy shore than at any other place in the world.

Kouchibouguac National Park, in New Brunswick, protects a rare and fragile coastal and beach ecosystem. It includes one of the most beautiful white-sand beaches in Canada, on a long barrier island in the warm waters of the Northumberland Strait.

Parks of the Prairie Provinces

Manitoba's Riding Mountain National Park has a resident herd of bison in its grasslands and a special camp of tepees where First Nations People tell visitors about the trees and plants that grow in the park. This park, with 650 streams and nearly 2,000 lakes and ponds, is known for its great variety of bird and animal life, including 160 species of nesting birds, 3,500 elk, and 1,000 black bears. Beavers create habitats for waterbirds and meadows where elk can browse.

Although it is not a park, Churchill, Manitoba, is known as the polar bear capital of the world, with 1,300-pound (590-kilogram) bears living close to the city, as well as beluga whales plunging in the waters of Churchill River. The area is covered in tundra flowers in the spring and fall, and evergreen forests called taiga grow nearby.

Manitoba has many polar bears.

Prince Albert National Park, in Saskatchewan, covers nearly 1 million acres (404,700 hectares) of wilderness forests and grasslands, cut by 1,500 lakes and streams. More than 230 species of birds have been seen there, along with gray wolves, caribou, and bison. In the same province, Grasslands National Park is a sanctuary protecting some of the last untouched prairie in North America, as well as a wild eroded landscape that escaped scraping by glaciers.

Wood Buffalo National Park, on the border between Alberta and the Northwest Territories, is the breeding ground of the rare whooping crane, a 5-foot (1.5-m)-tall bird. Canada's largest national park was originally set aside to protect the last free-ranging herd of wood bison, a larger variety of the American buffalo. These bison are the largest land mammals in Canada.

Rocky Mountain and Pacific Coast Parks

Four national parks—Banff, Jasper, Yoho, and Kootenay—preserve 11 percent of Canada's Rocky Mountains. The parks cover more than 7,800 square miles (20,200 sq km) of the Rockies and include some of Canada's most famous landmarks—Lake Louise, hot springs, the Columbia Icefield glaciers, and the magnificent ridgeline of Jasper's mountains. Yoho, the smallest of these parks, has twenty-two peaks that are more than 10,000 feet (3,048 m) high. Mountain animals such as bighorn sheep, mountain goats, moose, deer, and elk live here. Wolves and grizzly bears live in the more remote regions, and golden eagles soar overhead.

Below: **Mountain goats in British Columbia**
Below right: **A bighorn sheep**

With no roads or marked trails, Gwaii Haanas Reserve, off the coast of British Columbia, can be reached only by boat or floatplane. Here, bald eagles hunt for fish, to feed chicks in their 6-foot (1.8-m) nests, and peregrine falcon fly in at speeds of 100 miles (160 km) per hour. Colorful starfish lie in tidal pools beneath a majestic shoreline of 200-foot (61-m) spruce trees. This land on the Queen Charlotte Islands became a park reserve after the native Haida people protested that logging was stripping the area of its ancient trees. One section protects a stand of rare Haida-carved burial poles.

In the far north, Ivvavik National Park often has snow into July, melting next to patches of bright wildflowers. The only roads to the park are animal tracks, perhaps those of a grizzly bear, or hoofprints of some of the 150,000 caribou that live there. Flocks of snow geese turn the air white, and great shaggy musk oxen roam the tundra. This is a land of hardy, low-growing plants that can survive on ground that never thaws more than a few inches deep. Inuit people who live in the park are allowed to hunt and fish as their families have for generations. They are part of the ecosystem of this tundra.

Colorful starfish and other sea creatures are plentiful in the waters of Gwaii Haanas Reserve.

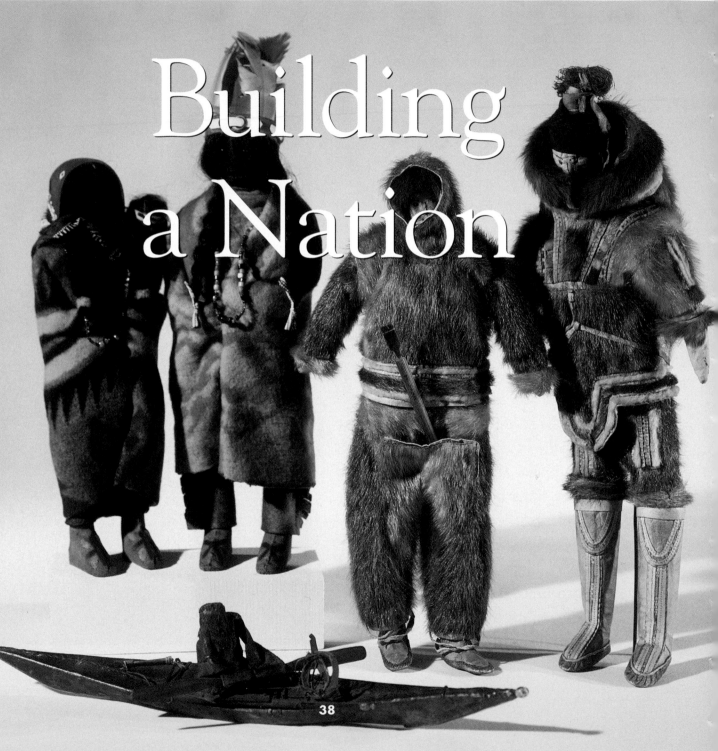

Building a Nation

M ANY PEOPLE IN THE UNITED STATES DON'T KNOW much about their neighbor but, like the United States, Canada has a rich and varied history. It has its own heroes and its own tales of westward expansion. The people of its First Nations have stories to tell too.

Canada's very first people were Asians who crossed over the land bridge that once connected Alaska with Siberia, in Russia. The next large wave of newcomers came thousands of years later, in the 1500s, when European explorers arrived in search of a quicker route to China, and stayed to trade with the local residents for their rich bounty of beaver furs.

Old wars between England and France took on new life in the new land, as the two empires battled for control of North America. England

Opposite: **A model kayak and dolls in traditional Inuit clothing**

ARCTIC OCEAN

coastline today

ASIA

ancient coastline

NORTH AMERICA

PACIFIC OCEAN

ATLANTIC OCEAN

Land Bridges to North America 18,000 years ago

Maximum extent of ice cap with (later) ice-free corridor
Possible migration routes of Asians to North America

won, but France left a legacy of its own culture, and the descendants of French people still dominate the land along the Saint Lawrence River. Later, thousands of immigrants from central Europe added new colors and flavors to the mix, and, finally, a railroad connected the east and the west—a great iron belt that held it all together.

The First Peoples Arrive

Most scientists now think that the first people in Canada were probably Asian hunters following herds of wild game across a narrow piece of land that once connected Asia and North America. Over the next several thousand years, small groups of people continued to cross and eventually fanned out over all of North and South America. Although many went south into warmer lands, some stayed to hunt the abundant animals of the northern forests and frozen tundra.

In Canada, the first people to settle the cold north lived mostly by hunting seals and walrus. They are called the Pre-Dorset peoples, and they had reached the eastern part of the Canadian Arctic by 1000 B.C. Their tools and campsites have been found in Newfoundland and elsewhere.

By 800 B.C., another people, called the Dorset, had developed their own culture in the eastern Arctic and in Newfoundland. They too were hunters and fishers, who used tools and other implements made of chipped stone and bone. They lived in sod houses, built partly underground and covered with grass. In summer, they used tents made of animal hides. The tools they used to scrape and tan these hides have

The Beothuk

In Newfoundland, the Dorsets seem to have been followed by another group—the Beothuk, who lived on the island until after the Europeans came. Organized groups of related families lived inland in the winter, in tepees called *mamateeks*, and hunted deer and caribou. In spring and summer, they moved to the coast and lived on seals and salmon.

The Beothuk covered themselves with a mixture of fat and red ocher from local soils, for religious reasons and also as a way to keep mosquitoes and other insects away. Settlers called them "Red Indians," and some people think this is how Native Americans came to be called "red men." The last Beothuk, Nancy Shawanahdit, died in 1829.

been found by archaeologists—scientists who study the artifacts left by early people. Archaeologists have also found ornaments, which the Dorsets made of wood, bone, and ivory, and quarries where they obtained stone to make lamps. Their civilization disappeared by about A.D. 1200. No one knows where they went, or whether they simply died out or blended with later groups.

Another group of people began moving east from Alaska about A.D. 900. These were the Thule, hunters whose culture was more highly developed. They established permanent winter communities along the shore, building houses of sod, whalebones, and skins. When traveling in search of food, they built igloos of snow as temporary shelter. They hunted whales, seals, walrus, polar bear, fish, and shellfish. They hunted and fished from one-person boats covered in animal skin, called *kayaks*. Open, skin-covered boats that held several people were called *umiaks*.

The umiaks used today are skin-covered boats based on those of the ancient Thule civilization.

The bright kayaks people use today for sport are based on these early Thule boats.

Although the modern world has changed it, Thule culture still survives among the Inuit and other peoples who live in the Arctic. Modern Arctic cultures, such as the Inuit, are thought to stem from these earlier people and their way of life. The Inuit culture began to develop about A.D. 1600 and is now found in six separate but similar groups. Five of these

A historical depiction of the Inuit people and culture

groups still hunt whale, seal, walrus, and fish for food. The sixth, the Caribou Inuit, live inland and hunt caribou.

South of the harsh, cold lands of the Dorset, Thule, and Inuit, other peoples began to occupy the more temperate parts of what would become Canada. Evidence has shown they were of a different origin from the peoples that settled the frozen north. Much of Alaska, British Columbia, Saskatchewan, and the Northwest Territories was settled by the Na-Dene peoples, which include the Athabascan, Tlingit, and Haida groups. The Haida were not only great traders, but also skilled artists who created beautiful carved totems and wooden boxes.

A Haida mask

Haida mortuary poles created in the nineteenth century honor high-ranking people.

Elsewhere, people of the Algonquin tribe and its subgroups lived in much of the Canadian Shield and Atlantic Coast area. The Huron, for example, lived in the area around Montreal. The Iroquois had a smaller space south of the Saint Lawrence River and into New England and northern New York. All these tribes were constantly competing and often fighting over the best hunting and fishing grounds.

Probably about 982, although the exact date is unknown, a Viking explorer known as Eric the Red sailed west from Greenland to Baffin Island. He did not stay, but he wrote about his adventures. His son, Leif Eriksson, later sailed west and in his journals described a place called Markland and another called Vinland. While no one knows for sure where Markland and Vinland were, scientists have found the remains of a Viking settlement at L'Anse Aux Meadows on the northwest tip of Newfoundland. They think it is the earliest European settlement in the New World. That settlement lasted only about a year before the Vikings were driven off by the native people.

Leif Eriksson Discovers America **by Christian Krohg**

By the mid-1500s, the spices, silk cloth, and gold of China and India were so important to European merchants that they competed fiercely to find a

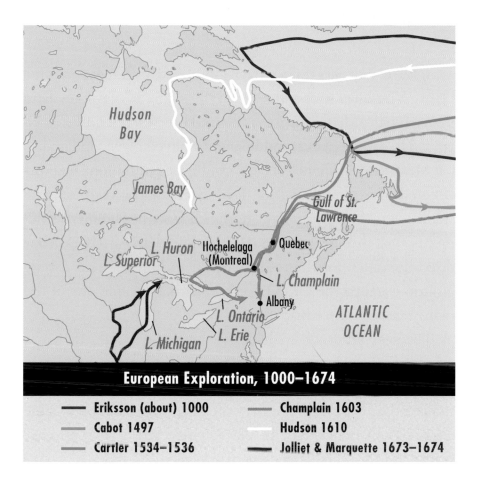

European Exploration, 1000–1674

— Eriksson (about) 1000

— Cabot 1497

— Cartier 1534–1536

— Champlain 1603

— Hudson 1610

— Jolliet & Marquette 1673–1674

faster and cheaper route to the Far East. The overland caravans that brought these goods were slow and dangerous. In addition, they could carry only a limited amount. A sea route would allow the merchants to become fabulously rich, and Europeans would have a plentiful supply of the luxuries they wanted from Asia.

The Portuguese searched for a sea route around Africa, and the British and French sent their explorers west to look for a route around the world to China and India. The great age of exploration was born.

John Cabot, an Italian navigator hired by England's King Henry VII, sailed west and reached the shores of Newfoundland in his ship the *Matthew* in 1497. He and his crew of eighteen men landed in several places, and England claimed Newfoundland.

Meanwhile, fishers from several European nations had discovered the abundance of fish, particularly cod, on the shallow continental shelf offshore. They set up summer settlements on the nearest land—Newfoundland—where they dried the catch for the return voyage to Europe. This fishing ground is called the Grand Banks. Fishing became one of the main reasons for settling the east coast of Canada.

Jacques Cartier, a French explorer, was also looking for a new route to China when he sailed into the Saint Lawrence River on his second voyage, in 1535. He stopped at a camp called Stadacona, on a part of the river the First Nations People called *Quebec*, which means "the place where the river narrows." Cartier set up a small fort there, then sailed 165 miles (265 km) farther up the river to the Huron village of Hochelaga.

Powerful rapids kept Cartier from going any farther, but he climbed the mountain behind the village and named it *Mont Réal* (Mount Royal). From the top, he saw the wide river

Before Montreal

When Jacques Cartier visited it in 1535, the Huron village of Hochelaga had forty to fifty substantial houses built of wood and skins. The village was surrounded by a triple palisade—three walls of logs—to protect the people from attack by the fierce Iroquois.

But when Samuel de Champlain came in 1603, the village had disappeared. Villages were often moved after a few years because of disease from accumulated human waste or because the soil was worn out. Today, the city of Montreal stands on the site of Hochelaga.

Samuel de Champlain

The daring French explorer Samuel de Champlain made his first trip up the Saint Lawrence River in 1603, going on to explore the area south of the river, well into what is now the U.S. state of Vermont. The huge lake that lies between New York, Vermont, and Canada was named Lake Champlain in his honor. After returning to France to raise money for his venture, Champlain returned to Canada in 1608 and founded the city of Quebec as a fur-trading post. By the time he died in 1635, Quebec was still only a village of 300 settlers, but its survival was due to Champlain. Under his leadership, the people overcame hunger, disease, attacks by the Iroquois and the British, as well as lack of support from France.

continuing off to the west, but he could not follow it because of the rapids. To this day, the part of the river that stopped Cartier is called *Lachine Rapids* (China Rapids).

The Lachine Rapids also stopped Samuel de Champlain, the next French explorer to sail up the Saint Lawrence River, in 1603. Champlain returned in 1608 and started a small settlement at Quebec. It struggled on and became a trade center, trading with the Indians for furs, particularly beaver skins. Beaver pelts were prized in Europe, where they were made into expensive hats, so the fur trade grew in importance. Traders began to travel farther and farther into the wilderness to find native trappers instead of waiting for the trappers to bring the pelts into the village. These fur trappers and traders were called *coureurs de bois*.

In 1627, in order to control the fur trade, the king of France created a private company called the Company of One Hundred Associates. The company actually ruled the lives of the settlers and traders. Along with traders, missionaries came from France to spread the Roman Catholic faith among the First Peoples. The fur trade and missionary work led Paul de Chomedey, Sieur de Maisonneuve, to settle at the foot of Mount Royal in 1642. He named his new town Ville-Marie de Montréal after the mountain that Cartier had named earlier. Farther west than Quebec and closer to the wilderness sources of furs, it soon became the center of the fur trade and commerce.

Soon after he started his colony at Quebec, Champlain realized that the major First Nations groups in the area—the Algonquin, the Huron, and the Iroquois—were often at war with one another. He decided to make a treaty with the Algonquin and Huron and join them in fighting the Iroquois. From the 1640s until 1701, the French and their allies fought the Iroquois.

While the French were trying to establish a monopoly in the fur trade, the English were also interested in this rich wilderness. They sent trappers and fur traders by ship into Hudson Bay and set up trading posts at the mouths of the rivers that emptied into the bay. Because it was easier to bring the pelts downriver in a canoe than haul them overland, the English began to control trade with the peoples of the First Nations.

In 1670, the king of England set up a company to compete with the French for the fur trade. It was called the Hudson's Bay Company, and it is still in business today, with department stores in most major Canadian cities. The king gave the Hudson's Bay Company land that encompassed what is now most of northern Quebec and Ontario, most of Saskatchewan, all of Manitoba, and large parts of Alberta and the Northwest Territories. In 1869, the Canadian Confederation bought that land from the company to create those provinces and territories.

A Hudson's Bay Company department store in Vancouver today

French Explorers in North America

French explorers and settlers were among the first Europeans to see much of Canada and the United States. Louis Jolliet explored the upper Saint Lawrence River and the Great Lakes region. He also teamed up with Jacques Marquette, a French priest, to explore the Mississippi River as far as the Arkansas River. René-Robert Cavelier, Sieur de La Salle, found a way to go from the Great Lakes to the Mississippi and Ohio Rivers in the early 1670s. He explored the Mississippi to its mouth on the Gulf of Mexico in 1682.

Almost from the beginning, France and England fought with each other for the control of North America, establishing colonies wherever they could. The rich fishing on the Grand Banks led the English to enforce the claim John Cabot had made for them when he landed in Newfoundland. Before he settled Quebec, Champlain had started a colony for France at Port Royal in Acadia, now Annapolis Royal, Nova Scotia. The French colony there had struggled on, creating farms in the Annapolis Valley. From there, the French spread out to establish farms in other parts of Nova Scotia and Prince Edward Island, which they irrigated and fertilized with a clever system of tidal dikes.

In the late 1600s and early 1700s, England and France went to war in Europe, and that struggle soon spread

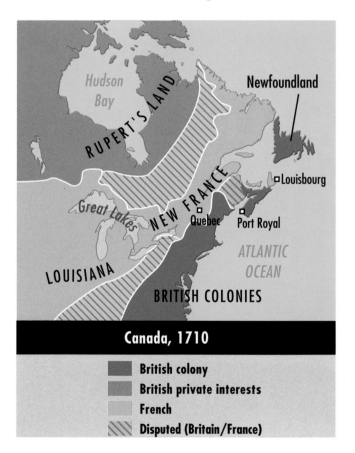

Canada, 1710

- British colony
- British private interests
- French
- Disputed (Britain/France)

to their American colonies. In 1710, British colonists from New England captured the old Acadian settlement of Port Royal in Nova Scotia. When the war in Europe finally ended, as part of its settlement France gave Britain the rights to Hudson Bay, Newfoundland, and Acadia, now called Nova Scotia.

But control of the Saint Lawrence River was the secret to control of North America. The French still held the great fortress of Louisbourg, on Cape Breton Island, from which they protected the sea routes leading into the river. In 1758, British colonists from New England seized Louisbourg and then went on to capture the city of Quebec in 1759. In 1760, British generals James Murray and Jeffrey Amherst defeated France's Chevalier de Levis and captured the last French stronghold—Montreal. New France was gone. The only North American lands left to France were the two tiny islands of Saint Pierre and Miquelon, just off Newfoundland.

The leaders of the French colony went back to France, leaving behind the ordinary settlers, called *habitants*. In 1774, the British passed the Quebec Act, allowing the habitants to keep their governmental and legal forms and their Roman Catholic religion. It was an unusual move in those times, when personal liberties—especially those of people who had lost a war—were not highly valued.

The rebellion in the thirteen British colonies—the American Revolution—created problems for the British in Canada too. The new United States began to look north, hoping that the French living there under British rule would join in the revolt.

The death of General Richard Montgomery during the American Revolution

Tories, or Loyalists, on their way to Canada during the American Revolution

On November 13, 1775, Americans captured Montreal, led by General Richard Montgomery. Another army, under General Benedict Arnold, attacked Quebec, but the French did not help them as they had expected. Arnold retreated to Montreal, and both armies went back to the United States. The British then tried to defeat the revolt in the colonies from their base in Canada, and the valley around Lake Champlain became a battleground.

Meanwhile, many British residents of the thirteen American colonies remained loyal to the king and had to leave America when the revolution began. They moved to the nearest British settlements—many going to Nova Scotia and New Brunswick—where they quickly fit into life in the cities of Fredericton, Saint John, Halifax, and many other smaller towns. In New England, British loyalists were called Tories, but Canadians called them Loyalists. Most were well-off merchants and government officials who quickly became leaders in their new communities.

For a century after U.S. independence, there were tensions between Canada and the United States. When the War of 1812 broke out between Britain and America, the Champlain Valley was again the scene of battle. In the United States, there was even talk of an invasion of Canada, but the war ended first. An attempt to settle the border between Canada and the United States in the 1840s led to more talk and bluster about invasion.

The borders seethed during the 1830s and 1840s, with secret societies promoting expansion of the U.S. borders. At the same time, people north of the border were unhappy with the restrictions of British rule in Canada. Several small rebellions in the late 1830s were easily put down, but they caused the British government to take notice of this discontent.

In 1840, Britain passed the Act of Union and renamed the province of Quebec Lower Canada and the lands to the west Upper Canada. The capital of the new state was in Kingston in English-speaking Upper Canada, now

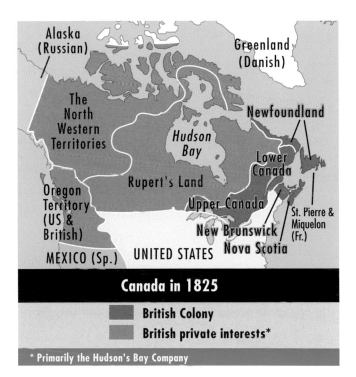

Canada in 1825

British Colony

British private interests*

* Primarily the Hudson's Bay Company

The Mounties

In 1874, 275 recruits of the Northwest Mounted Police, as they were called then, were sent from Manitoba on a westward march to bring law and order to the northwest. Today's Highway 13, called the Redcoat Trail, is close to their original route. Some of the early posts along this trail have been restored as historic sites.

In 1999, the Royal Canadian Mounted Police—the Mounties—celebrated their origins as a nationwide force with a reenactment of their historic ride west, when they built frontier posts and established friendly relations with the First Nations Peoples who lived there. Canada's only training academy for recruits is in Regina, the capital of Saskatchewan.

Ontario. Because there was disagreement with the United States over Oregon and the exact boundary between the two countries, Canada's capital was moved away from the border, to Ottawa. Ottawa is still the capital of Canada today.

The combined lands of Upper and Lower Canada were called the Province of Canada. They were given an elected legislature with limited powers, but their governors were still appointed by the British king.

Britain and Canada both supported the Southern states during the American Civil War, and the situation along the border once again became tense. U.S. politicians blustered about Canada, but no battles were fought.

Based on discussions in Prince Edward Island in 1864, the British North America Act was passed by the British

Parliament in 1867, to strengthen the Canadian colonies. This law combined Ontario, Quebec (now given back its old name), Nova Scotia, and New Brunswick into a confederation called the Dominion of Canada. The Canadians were allowed more self-government, but Britain was still in control.

Manitoba (in the middle west), British Columbia (on the West Coast), Prince Edward Island (off the East Coast), and the Arctic lands of the Northwest Territories all joined the confederation in the early 1870s.

One of Canada's biggest problems was its lack of good roads and communications among the provinces, which now stretched all across the country. Roads were muddy paths, and the wet boggy land of the great Canadian Shield made building roads very difficult.

By the 1880s, however, railroad building was a well-established technology, and the monumental job of creating a railroad across Canada began. Completed in 1885, it proved to be the thread that would link all the separate provinces together.

From the middle of the 1800s until the beginning of the 1900s, Americans poured into the West, settling the whole continent. As they went west, they not only went into Texas and California, but began to head north, particularly into the plains area of Canada.

Rivalry with the United States and fears that these U.S. settlers would claim western Canada—as they had done in Mexico—led Canada to encourage Europeans to immigrate to the lands west of Quebec. The new railroad became a way to get this new wave of immigrants to the mostly empty interior.

At the end of the 1800s, the government began an aggressive program to invite immigrants, many of them from eastern Europe. After landing by boat in Quebec or Montreal, they were quickly put on trains to the West, where they and their children formed a new piece of the huge Canadian jigsaw puzzle. These new settlers on the prairies, many of whom had been farmers in their European homelands, began to grow huge quantities of wheat and other grains. These crops were shipped by the new railroad to the grain elevators of Montreal and by boat to markets beyond.

Wounded men of the Riel Rebellion

Rebellion in the West

The west into which Canada invited the European immigrants was not entirely uninhabited. The *Métis*, descendants of French trappers and traders who had married native women, joined with First Nations Peoples in Saskatchewan in an armed revolt against the Canadian government. They claimed rights to lands in the west, as well as other rights as Canadian citizens, and their anger crystallized into an organized revolt under the leadership of Louis Riel.

Even today, people disagree on whether Riel was a patriot or a traitor. But after two months of bitter fighting, Riel and his Métis and native army were defeated. Riel was accused of treason, tried, and hanged as a traitor. This Northwest Rebellion was the last military conflict on Canadian soil.

The Twentieth Century

In World War I (1914–1918), 600,000 Canadian troops fought alongside the British armed forces. The Canadian Corps, a specially trained elite fighting unit, is credited with victories in at least two major assaults, but Canadian losses were high. Ten percent of all Canadian fighting men never came home, and 20 percent were wounded.

Canadian soldiers in France during World War I

Their sacrifice not only helped win the war, however, but it earned Canada a voice in military decisions and—after the war—greater self-government. Canada was recognized as a separate nation, leading to the Statute of Westminster. Passed by the British Parliament in 1931, the statute made Canada and other dominions of the British Empire "partner nations." This officially made Canada equal in status to Britain, Australia, New Zealand, and other major members of the British Commonwealth. In that same year, Norway gave up its claim to the Sverdrup Islands in the Arctic, recognizing them as Canadian land.

Canadian soldiers returning home from Europe following World War II

A Vital Air Station

The airstrip at Gander, Newfoundland, was most important to the steady stream of troops and supplies that were flown to Europe from Canada and the United States during World War II. Nearly every flight to Europe stopped to refuel at Gander, which had the closest fog-free runways to Britain. After the war, in 1949, Newfoundland became the tenth province of Canada.

In World War II (1939–1945), Canada took even greater strides toward the place it now holds as an important nation of the world. More than 1 million Canadians served in the armed forces, with over 40,000 casualties. Canadian factories turned out equipment, and food from Canadian farms fed Allied troops in the field.

Canada joined the United Nations when it was formed after World War II, and later joined NATO, along with the United States and other free nations opposing the spread of communism throughout the world.

With the rise of the Liberal Party to power in the 1960s, Canada, while maintaining defensive agreements with the United States, began to be more independent in its role in world affairs. Not only did Canada not always agree with U.S. foreign policy, but Canada wanted to be thought of as a separate place, with an identity of its own. During the Vietnam War, Canada welcomed young men from the United States who wanted to avoid being drafted. Many of those who moved north to escape military service stayed, becoming Canadian citizens.

Resettlement

Few colonists wanted to move to the cold, inhospitable land of the Northwest Territories, so that region was left to the Inuit, who lived nomadic lives. But in the 1950s and 1960s, the government made them settle into communities, so that it would be easier to provide them with schooling and health care.

Also, having actual towns in these remote northern areas helped the Canadian government to back up its claims to the lands of the high Arctic. During the cold war, the Soviet Union wanted to control the Arctic and claimed that some of the land was theirs. Having Canadian citizens living in towns there made it easier for Canada to prove it was Canadian land.

In Newfoundland, at about this time, many people lived in small towns called "outports." These were mainly fishing villages, where boats were the only way to get anywhere because it was difficult to build roads over the remote, rugged land between villages. And because everyone there

An abandoned outport community in Newfoundland

fished, they were more used to traveling by boat.

However, the government decided that people should not be living in these small, remote towns and forced thousands of people to move to larger towns in Newfoundland. Some people put their houses on big barges and floated them to nearby towns, but most had to leave the homes their families had lived in for generations.

Even today, you can find ghost towns that were once thriving outport communities on the edge of the sea and meet people who grew up in them.

Constitutional Separation

Queen Elizabeth II traveled to Canada in 1982 to sign the Constitution Act, cutting the last control of the British Parliament over Canada's government. Until then, if Canada wanted to amend its Constitution, the government had to get approval from the British Parliament. Now Canada could change its own Constitution. This was a major goal of Canadian premier Pierre Elliott Trudeau, whose French supporters in Quebec saw the old system as a major example of how Britain and English-speaking people (Anglophones) controlled Canada's future. But many others supported this separation too.

Queen Elizabeth II signs the Constitution Act as Prime Minister Pierre Trudeau watches approvingly.

Quebec Grows Restless

From the first days of British control, after France gave up its claims to Canada, the British allowed the French residents to keep their language, religion, laws, and systems of government. But economic growth in French Quebec, which is mostly rural and still strongly controlled by the Catholic Church, always lagged behind British Canada.

In the 1960s, growing prosperity and a leader named René Lévesque awakened the province to a more modern way of life. But along with modernization came unrest, with Quebec residents growing dissatisfied with their relationship with the rest of the Canada. The French-speaking people (Francophones) of Quebec felt that their culture was being threatened by Canada's Anglophone majority. They sought special protection for their language and French heritage.

René Lévesque

The first voices of separation were heard, and British Canada responded by promoting bilingualism (the use of both the French and the English language) throughout the country. In 1963, violence broke out, led by a radical political organization called the *Front de Libération du Québec* (FLQ). People were kidnapped—even killed—by this group before their revolutionary tactics were stopped by the government and rejected by the people of Quebec. Quebec and Canada, they promised, would solve their problems the Canadian way, by discussion and compromise.

A new political party, *Le Parti Québécois*, formed in 1968 to work toward separating Quebec from Canada, won control of the province's government in 1976. Separatists in Quebec—people who want the province to become a separate country—grew louder and louder. To try to resolve the matter, representatives of Canada's national government met with the separatists to draft the Meech Lake Accord, an effort to ease their fears about losing their French identity. This accord sought to give Quebec a special constitutional status as "a distinct society," but it failed to be approved by all the provinces,

Language Police

One of the most difficult positions for the Quebec government to explain is the province's language laws. Designed to protect and preserve the use of French in Quebec, these laws have gone to extremes that even their supporters have a hard time defending. By law, all outdoor signs must be in French only. Businesses such as The Bay, stores of the Hudson's Bay Company, must change their company names if they do business in Quebec.

Indoor signs may be in both French and English, but the French lettering must be at least twice as large as the English lettering. If the colors are not the same, the color of the French words must be "stronger." In 1998, restaurants in Montreal's Chinatown closed in protest against this ruling, which prohibited them from having any signs in Chinese. A special force, which people call "tongue troopers," has been established to enforce these laws.

as required by law. A second attempt at an accord also failed, and bitterness grew on both sides.

In order to keep Canada united, the three major political parties agreed in 1992 to make constitutional changes allowing Quebec a separate voice. But Québécois still pushed for separation. In October 1995, a secession referendum (a vote to decide if Quebec would leave Canada) failed to pass. But the vote was close, as was a second one in 1998. In 1998, however, Canada's Supreme Court ruled that Quebec cannot secede without the rest of Canada's consent, even if a majority of the province approves the referendum.

Most Canadians feel that losing Quebec would seriously damage Canada. If Quebec were to keep its borders as a separate country (and it is very unlikely that Canada would allow this), the four Atlantic provinces would be cut off from the rest of Canada. Also, a new country in the middle would break the rail, road, and water routes that link the country together. And certainly, there would be serious arguments over who owned the rights to the hydroelectric power generated by the waters flowing into Hudson and James Bays. This is an important source of electricity for all of eastern Canada—and for part of the United States too.

First Nations Peoples living in Quebec worry about their future if Quebec becomes a separate country. They fear that their ancient culture will be destroyed and that they will be forced to speak French and adopt French ways. They point to Quebec's poor record of respecting their traditions, language, and way of life. And, they ask, if Quebec has a right to vote to separate from Canada, why can't we vote to be independent from Quebec?

It is likely that the question of an independent Quebec will remain unresolved for a long time, with separatists continuing to push for new votes. This creates an uncertain future for businesses and industry in Quebec, because outside companies are afraid to invest there. They fear that if Quebec becomes a country, the new government would need money so badly that it would impose heavy taxes, especially on non-French-owned companies. Many Canadian and international businesses have already left the province, increasing both unemployment and the bitterness of the French separatists.

A Confederation of Differences

THE WAYS IN WHICH CANADA AND THE UNITED STATES are governed are one of the great distinctions between the two countries. Each nation's system is rooted deep in its history and rose from its earliest formation. While the U.S. government is based on the British system of laws and British political philosophy, its self-government came by revolution. As a result, the leaders had to come up with a new form of government. Because they had rejected the British king as the head of government, there was no executive to administer the laws. The leaders of the new government had to invent one, so they created the presidency, with a separate executive branch of government.

How the Government Grew

Canada had no revolution. Instead, Canadian people, over many years, put pressure on the British ruler and Parliament to give them more control over their own lives. Under this pressure, Britain and its king or queen gradually gave up parts of their power and began to direct the government of Canada less and less.

Opposite: **Ottawa's City Hall is a very modern building.**

The changing of the guard in front of the Parliament building in Ottawa

A New Flag for Canada

Until 1965, Canada did not have its own flag. It used the traditional flag of all the British dominions and colonies, with the British "Union Jack" in one corner. But in 1965, a dramatic new flag was raised in Ottawa and all over Canada, featuring a bright red maple leaf on a wide white center stripe, with a red stripe on either side. The maple leaf had been a national symbol for a long time. This strong hardwood tree provides lumber and sweet maple syrup and colors the hillsides bright shades of red and orange in the fall.

In Britain, the government was run by a parliamentary system, which is quite different from the system that developed in the United States. Since Canadian government evolved slowly as it became more independent of Britain, its system of government remained close to that of its parent country.

In England, at the time when Canada and the United States were forming, the king or queen was the head of government—the executive. The monarchs inherited the crown from their parents or other relatives and could not be removed from office by the vote of the people. Voters elected representatives to the House of Commons, the legislature where laws are made. These members of the House of Commons belonged to many political parties, but the party with the most members elected to the Commons chose one person—the prime minister—to run the government. In a parliamentary system, if members of Parliament don't like the way the prime minister is doing the job, he or she can be removed from office by a

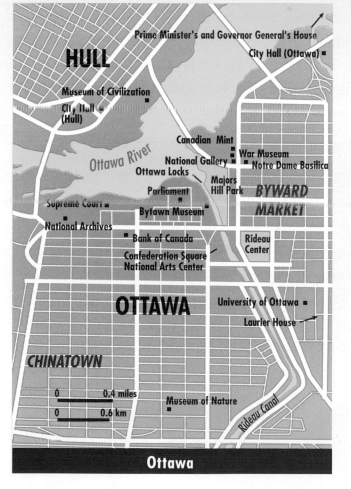

Ottawa

Ottawa: Did You Know This?

Explorer Samuel de Champlain first reached the site of Ottawa in 1613. The town was later named Bytown, for John By, an engineer who built the Rideau Canal in the nineteenth century. Today, Ottawa is a technology center and home to several colleges and universities, in addition to being the nation's capital.

Metropolitan Population: 1,010,498

Founded: 1827

Became Capital: 1857

Altitude: 339 feet (103 m)

Average Temperature in July: 65°F (18°C)

Average Temperature in January: 9°F (−13°C)

"vote of no confidence" in the House of Commons. In Canada, the voters can remove a prime minister from office by voting his or her party out of office in Parliament in the next election.

The head of Canada's government today is the queen (or king) of the United Kingdom of Great Britain and Northern Ireland, but that monarch's powers are mostly ceremonial. In the beginning of British rule, the Crown appointed a governor-general to govern Canada, who had most of the powers of the monarch. As time went by, these powers were cut back one by one and given to Canada's House of Commons. Today, although the queen still appoints the governor-general, Canada's prime minister tells her who to appoint—and the job is only ceremonial.

Britain's Queen Elizabeth II visiting Canada

NATIONAL GOVERNMENT OF CANADA

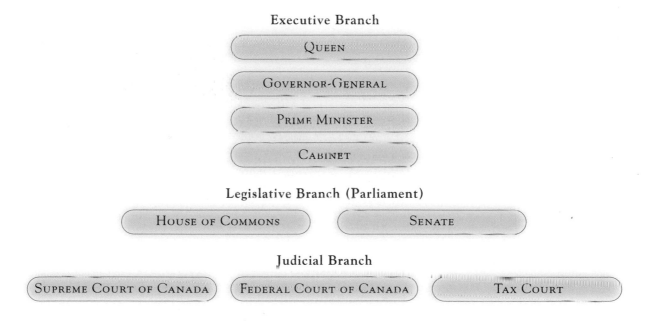

Executive Branch

- Queen
- Governor-General
- Prime Minister
- Cabinet

Legislative Branch (Parliament)

- House of Commons
- Senate

Judicial Branch

- Supreme Court of Canada
- Federal Court of Canada
- Tax Court

The Executive Branch

After an election, the political party that wins the most seats in the House of Commons becomes the "governing," or "ruling" party. At their first meeting, they elect a member of their party—usually its leader—to be prime minister. The three leading parties today are the Liberal, the Progressive Conservative, and the New Democratic Parties.

The prime minister chooses people from the governing party to be members of the Cabinet. All Cabinet members must also be elected members of the House of Commons or the Senate, and each one is head of a government department.

Pierre Trudeau

Born in Montreal in 1919, Pierre Elliott Trudeau was educated at the University of Montreal before going to Harvard University in the United States and graduate schools in Paris and London. At age thirty-one, he began his political career. Fifteen years later, he entered federal government and was soon appointed minister of justice. Almost immediately, he was elected to lead Canada's Liberal Party. He served as prime minister from 1968 to 1979 and from 1980 to 1984, working hard to gain rights for Quebec's French population while trying to keep them a part of Canada. He opposed separation and worked against the referendum votes that would have led to it. He worked to promote the Canadian Constitution of 1982, hoping to satisfy Quebec with its move away from British influence.

The prime minister and the Cabinet lead the government and tell government employees what programs and policies to follow. This is called the executive branch. The Canadian executive branch, headed by the prime minister and the cabinet, is part of the legislative branch. In the United States, the executive branch is totally separate.

The Legislative Branch

No Postage Needed

When Canadians want to write to their MP, all they have to do is write the letter, address it, and put it in the mailbox. No stamps are needed.

In Canada, the real political power is in the legislature. It is *bicameral*, which means that there are two sections—the House of Commons and the Senate. The most powerful is the House of Commons, whose 301 members are called members of Parliament (MPs). The number of MPs may change to reflect population or political changes in Canada. All laws involving the raising or spending of money, as well as most of the important legislation, is passed by the House of Commons.

The two Canadian houses of Parliament are not equal. This is probably because the example they followed was the traditional British House of Lords, which was not elected by the people and had less power than the House of Commons.

Canada's Senate is made up of 105 members, chosen to represent different regions. Senators are not elected. Instead, they are appointed by the queen's representative, the governor-general. However, the prime minister tells the governor-general who to appoint. Senators can keep their job until they are seventy-five years old.

Speaker of the House Gib Parent addressing the House of Commons

The Senate Chamber of the Parliament building

The Question Period

Every day the House of Commons meets, forty-five minutes of the Parliament's time is set aside for the prime minister and the Cabinet to answer questions from the MPs. If the MPs are not happy with the answers, the Cabinet members and even the prime minister can lose their jobs.

The Senate cannot propose any law that involves the raising or spending of money. These must begin in the House of Commons. Although all laws must be approved by both houses, it is very rare that a bill passed by the House of Commons is not approved by the Senate. Sometimes the Senate amends (changes) a bill, in which case the amendment must be approved by the House of Commons too. Long-term studies of major problems are done by the Senate.

The Provinces

The federal government in Ottawa takes care of problems that affect all the provinces and territories. Canada is divided into ten provinces and three territories, and each of them has its own government. In many ways, these divisions are like the states of the United States. Each province and territory has its own government. They are closer to the daily life of the people that live within their boundaries, so these governments take care of issues that affect only their own people.

The government of each province is organized very much like that of the federal government of Canada. But instead of a legislative branch divided into a House of Commons and a Senate, there is only one house. These are called by different names—either the Legislative Assembly, the Provincial Parliament, or the House of Assembly. Quebec's provincial assembly is called the National Assembly.

Just as in the federal government, the political party that has the most votes in the Assembly elects one of its own members to head the government. The person elected is called the

The Parliament of
British Columbia

premier, and he or she appoints a council to help run the government. The premier and the council are the heads of the provincial executive branch.

The members of the Assembly are elected by the people of the province. The provincial assemblies pass all the laws needed to run the affairs of the province. They provide the money to run schools, they build and maintain roads, and they provide for the welfare of the people.

Each province also has a lieutenant-governor who represents the British monarch and serves as the ceremonial head of the executive branch. The lieutenant-governor is appointed by Canada's governor-general on the advice of the prime minister and has few powers or duties. The real power to run the departments of provincial governments is held by the premier and his or her council.

Canada's territories, which have smaller and widely scattered populations, are governed somewhat differently from provinces. While they have their own legislatures, their affairs are more closely governed from Ottawa. Their representatives work with the federal government in deciding what will happen in the territories. Many people in these areas work for the government as teachers or health-care professionals.

Local Government

Town and city government in Canada is controlled by the provincial assembly. People in towns and cities elect mayors and councils to operate the local government, but they have no source of tax money to pay the costs. The money to run the city and town governments comes from taxes collected by the province, which is then given back to the towns by the provincial assembly.

Provincial assemblies can refuse to allow towns and cities to do things they want to do. In the 1990s, for example, many towns and cities were forcibly joined together to make large municipalities. Many people in these towns did not want to become part of a bigger city, but they had no say in the matter.

Voting Rights

Any Canadian citizen who is at least eighteen years old can vote in national elections. Before every election, people called enumerators go from house to house gathering the names of people who are entitled to vote. They put these names on a list and give each voter an Elector Information Card. The card confirms that

Canadians standing in line to cast their ballots in provincial elections

the voter's name is on the list. On election day—called Polling Day—anyone who cannot get to the voting place can make special arrangements to cast their ballot. Voting in Canada is by secret ballot so that each person's decision is private.

The Rights of Canadians

Canadians are guaranteed most of the same rights that citizens of the United States have. While most of these rights have existed for many years, they were brought together in a law passed in 1982 called the Canadian Charter of Rights and Freedoms. The charter gives every Canadian the right to vote and participate in federal and provincial government; to have fair and equal access to the court system; to live and work anywhere they want to in Canada; and to enjoy freedom of religion, thought, speech, and the right to assemble in public meetings. The charter also protects the rights of the aboriginal peoples (people whose ancestors lived here before European settlers arrived) to the preservation of their cultures.

The Origins of Canada's Name

The name *Canada* originated with the early explorer, Jacques Cartier, who used the First Nations word *kanata*, which means "village." European mapmakers changed the spelling to *Canada*, using it to label all lands north of the Saint Lawrence River.

A Quick Look at Canada's Provinces

Alberta

Population: 2,847,000

Capital: Edmonton

Largest City: Edmonton

Edmonton is the home of the world's largest indoor shopping mall; the Calgary Stampede (below), held every July, is the world's largest rodeo.

British Columbia

Population: 4,010,000

Capital: Victoria

Largest City: Vancouver

British Columbia has rain forests as well as a desert; Canada's highest waterfall—Della Falls, 1,443 feet (440 m) high—is in British Columbia.

Manitoba

Population: 1,145,200

Capital: Winnipeg

Largest City: Winnipeg

Manitoba is known as the Land of 100,000 Lakes, but it actually has more. Winnipeg is the source of the name "Winnie the Pooh." Polar bears live so close to Manitoba's city of Churchill that they sometimes wander into town.

New Brunswick

Population: 762,000

Capital: Fredericton

Largest City: Saint John

New Brunswick has two official languages—French and English—and both are taught in public schools. More varieties of whales are found in greater numbers in New Brunswick's Bay of Fundy (below) than in any other place in the world.

Newfoundland

Population: 563,600
Capital: St. John's
Largest City: St. John's

Newfoundland has its own time zone, one half-hour ahead of the rest of the Atlantic provinces. St. John's is Canada's foggiest city, shrouded in thick fog an average of 121 days a year.

Nova Scotia

Population: 936,092
Capital: Halifax
Largest City: Halifax

Halifax has one of the finest natural harbors in the world. Survivors from the *Titanic* were brought to Halifax, and many of the dead are buried there.

Ontario

Population: 11,407,700
Capital: Toronto
Largest City: Toronto

Toronto has the most ethnically diverse population of any city in Canada.

Prince Edward Island

Population: 137,200
Capital: Charlottetown
Largest City: Charlottetown

Prince Edward Island is the smallest province in land area and in population.

Quebec

Population: 7,419,900
Capital: Quebec City
Largest City: Montreal

Quebec's only official language is French. Quebec City has the world's largest winter carnival, with ten days of festivities, snow sculptures, and competitions.

Saskatchewan

Population: 1,023,500
Capital: Regina
Largest City: Saskatoon

Saskatchewan produces more than half of Canada's wheat crop. It has more than 155,000 miles (250,000 km) of road surface, more than any other province.

Northwest Territories

Population: 40,300
Capital: Yellowknife
Largest City: Yellowknife

Canada's longest river—the Mackenzie—and its two largest lakes are in Northwest Territories.

Nunavut Territory

Population: 27,200
Capital: Iqaluit
Largest City: Iqaluit

Nunavut covers one-fifth of all the land in Canada and stretches across three time zones. None of Nunavut's twenty-eight towns has a road connecting it to the rest of Canada, and the entire territory has only 12 miles (20 km) of highway.

Yukon Territory

Population: 31,600
Capital: Whitehorse
Largest City: Whitehorse

North America's largest gold rush took place in Yukon's Klondike district in 1898. The coldest temperature ever recorded in North America was −81.4°F (−63°C) in the Yukon.

The federal government provides all Canadians with many services that people in some other countries must pay for by themselves. The Canadian philosophy is to provide equally for everyone, and let those who can afford it pay for the services through taxes. Instead of having their own health-insurance policies, all Canadians have a national health insurance that pays all their doctor and hospital bills.

Canadians do not all agree that this is the best system, however. Some Canadians who need major medical treatment travel to the United States, where they do not have to wait as long for treatment. Everyone agrees that the system is very expensive because of the high taxes needed to pay for it, but they like the fact that everyone is treated the same, and they agree that health-care standards are high.

Fifth graders of an Inuit community learn a song in school.

Several other services are provided to everyone by the government, too. Families with children receive payments under the Family Allowances Act, help is available for housing, disability and unemployment insurance are provided, and there are maternity benefits for women and pensions for retired people.

Education standards are very high. Each province sets its own qualifications for teachers and decides what subjects will be taught in its schools.

The campus of McGill University in Montreal

In most provinces, children must attend school from ages six through sixteen. Grades are kindergarten through grade twelve. Roman Catholic schools have their own school boards, but the government provides some of the money to operate the schools.

After high school, students may attend community colleges or one of Canada's more than fifty universities. These are supported by the government, so tuition is comparatively low. Work-study programs and government grants help students who cannot afford even these low rates to get a college education.

Language in Quebec's Schools

Parents of French ancestry can no longer choose whether their children will attend French-language schools or English-language schools. The French speakers in Quebec decided that allowing the choice of English schools was weakening the French language. In 1974, they voted to make French the official language of Quebec, and in 1979, the Supreme Court approved their decision. Most English-speaking people in Quebec can still send their children to English schools, but the law says that if your grandfather went to a French school, you must go to a French school, no matter which language your family now speaks at home. All children of immigrants must send their children to French-speaking schools.

How Canada
Earns a Living

CANADA'S ECONOMY IS AS LARGE AS ITS LAND AND AS varied as its population. Even though the country was in an economic recession through most of the 1990s, its gross national product (the value of all goods and services produced during a year) was the third-largest in the world. And these goods and services are produced by a workforce of only about 13.5 million people.

At the turn of the twentieth century, most Canadians worked in agriculture, fishing, mining, or forestry. As we enter the twenty-first century, about 75 percent of Canadian workers earn their living in the service industry. They work in banks, insurance companies, communications industries, government, schools, hospitals, tourism, and other service-related businesses. More than 15 percent of the workforce earns its living in manufacturing—most of them in Quebec province and southern Ontario, where automobile production is an important part of the economy. Only 4 percent of the people working in Canada are involved in agriculture, and the remaining 6 percent work in other jobs, such as forestry and construction.

Foreign Trade

Canada is one of the most important trading nations in the world. Canadians import goods and services valued at 169.5 billion Canadian dollars from abroad, and they export goods

Teams of mechanics assemble airplanes in this Ontario plant.

worth 195 billion Canadian dollars to foreign countries. More than half of the imports are machinery and transportation equipment, including cars and trucks.

More than 15 percent of Canada's workers have jobs in manufacturing. Many of these jobs involve the manufacture of cars, trucks, and automotive parts. One of the early developers of snowmobiles was the Bombardier Corporation in Quebec province, and the company is still an important part of the economy there. Other important manufactured goods are machines, telecommunications equipment, and a wide range of consumer goods.

Loonies and Toonies

Canada's currency is called the dollar. Bills are issued in values of 5, 10, 20, 50, and 100 dollars, and coins are worth 1, 5, 10, and 25 cents and 1 and 2 dollars.

Canada's one-dollar coin (right) is called a "Loonie" because it pictures a loon—a bird found in many parts of Canada. The loon is a waterbird that nests in secluded lakes and bays. It eats fish and can dive for long distances to catch them. Because of its solitary habits and preference for remote places, the loon has become a symbol of Canada's wilderness. The two-dollar coin, which features a polar bear, is called a "Toonie" because it is worth two Loonies.

How important Canada and the United States are to each other is illustrated dramatically in the trade between the two neighbors. Sixty-five percent of all goods imported into Canada come from the United States, and more than 81 percent of Canada's exports are sold to the United States. Canada's next most important trading partner is Japan. Canada imports 6.1 percent of its needs from Japan and sells that nation 4.6 percent of its exports. No other country has more than 3 percent of Canadian imports or exports.

Since 1989, the United States and Canada have had a free-trade agreement, and in 1992 Mexico joined its northern neighbors in signing the North American Free Trade Agreement (NAFTA). Under its terms, which took effect in 1994, all three countries agreed that within ten years they would eliminate taxes on goods bought and sold between them. Many people in Canada feel that the treaty hurt the Canadian economy and caused Canadian businesses to move to the United States. Others feel that getting rid of import taxes made Canadian-made goods more popular in the United States because they are cheaper than goods produced there. They feel the treaty has been good for Canada. No import or export taxes are imposed on goods shipped between these three countries today.

Canada's Resources

Canada has abundant mineral resources, and the mining and processing of those minerals provide many Canadians with jobs. Important minerals include nickel, bauxite (aluminum),

Canadian Imports*

United States	65.0%
Japan	6.1%
United Kingdom	2.6%
Mexico	2.2%
Germany	2.0%
All others	24.1%

*Does not total 100%.

Canadian Exports

United States	81.3%
Japan	4.6%
United Kingdom	1.5%
Germany	1.3%
All others	11.3%

An aerial view of iron ore pits in Labrador

iron ore, zinc, copper, lead, and gold. Petroleum and natural gas are also plentiful in Canada, and their sale accounts for more than 10 percent of the nation's exports.

As a large country with a small population, Canada has huge areas of forestland that provide it with an almost endless supply of wood. About

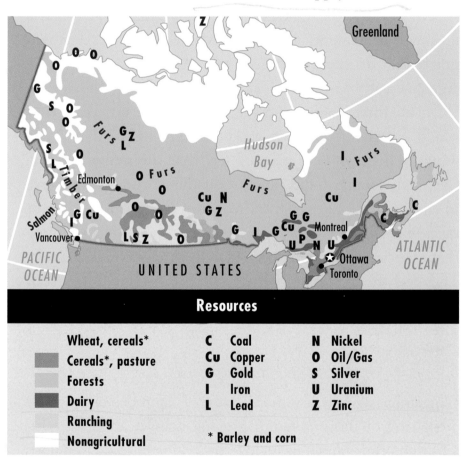

Resources

▨ Wheat, cereals*	C	Coal	N	Nickel
▨ Cereals*, pasture	Cu	Copper	O	Oil/Gas
▨ Forests	G	Gold	S	Silver
▨ Dairy	I	Iron	U	Uranium
▨ Ranching	L	Lead	Z	Zinc
▢ Nonagricultural			

* Barley and corn

54 percent of the country is made up of forests and woodland. Much of it is milled into finished lumber for export, mostly to the United States and Asia. Another large part is used to make paper, including newsprint. Lumber and timber operations are important to the economies of almost all the provinces except Prince Edward Island.

About 5 percent of Canada's exports are finished lumber, and an additional 5.7 percent are newsprint and pulp wood. Along the border between Canada and the United States, Canadian lumberyards import logs from the United States and process them into lumber products for sale back to the United States.

A forest partially cleared by the lumber industry

A hydroelectric dam on the Manicouagan River in Quebec

The increasing demand for energy in Canada and the United States has created many new jobs in Canada. More than 10 percent of Canadian exports are energy fuels, including crude petroleum, refined petroleum products, and natural gas. In Quebec province, huge dams and electricity-generating power plants have been built on the vast, wild rivers that flow into James Bay. Much of this electricity is sold to consumers in the United States.

What Canada Grows, Makes, and Mines

Agriculture (1996)

Wheat	23,024,000 metric tons
Barley	13,590,000 metric tons
Corn (maize)	7,000,000 metric tons

Manufacturing (1996; valued added in Canadian dollars)

Transportation equipment	$16,181,700,000
Electrical products	$12,570,700,000
Food	$10,556,600,000

Mining (1996)

Iron ore	36,030,000 metric tons
Zinc	1,187,829 metric tons
Copper	655,891 metric tons

Agriculture and Fishing

Agriculture is important to many Canadians, as a way of life and as their income. The rich plains of the western provinces produce enough wheat and other grains to feed Canada and export a large surplus. The area south of the Saint Lawrence River is also a major producer of dairy products and vegetables. Agriculture is important even in metropolitan Montreal, where the flower growers of the city of Laval grow many of the flowers and plants used throughout Canada all year long. Food products—especially wheat—grown in Canada make up more than 6.5 percent of exports.

Fishing has also been an important industry on the east and west coasts and the Great Lakes. In recent years, however, pollution and overfishing have drastically cut the number and variety of fish. On the west coast, salmon fishing has been an

Canadian fishers catching cod

important industry almost since the first settlements there. Dramatic declines in the catch have led Canadian fishers to claim that U.S. boats are catching Canadian fish and damaging their fisheries.

Off the eastern provinces along the Atlantic shore, huge factory ships from Russia, Japan, and Scandinavia have drained the best fishing areas. This overfishing led to regulations that closed important fishing grounds. Hundreds of fishers have had to sell their boats and find another way to make a living. In Newfoundland, a way of life more than 500 years old has been eliminated.

Tourism

One often-overlooked part of Canada's economy is tourism. More than 15 million tourists visited Canada in 1999. Many are attracted to exciting cities like Vancouver, Toronto, Montreal, and Halifax, while others are drawn to the wilderness and the magnificent scenery of both coasts.

Newfoundland offers the UNESCO World Heritage site of Gros Morne National Park, and, in nearby New Brunswick, special programs for visitors allow beginners to experience all sorts of outdoor adventures like kayaking, dogsledding, and hiking. In the West, the Canadian Rockies offer their untamed wildness. The Coast Mountains and Queen Charlotte Islands draw visitors to the northern rain forests and many water and other outdoor sports. Each summer, the waters of the West Coast's Inside Passage are filled with cruise ships, from which people can admire the dramatic shoreline. Even in the sparsely

settled north, the tundra and icebound lands offer unique adventures in sport fishing, hunting, and spectacular wildlife. Special events such as the Calgary Stampede—the world's biggest rodeo and wild west show—draw hundreds of thousands of visitors. Canada's landscape and wildlife are natural resources as valuable as its minerals.

Whale-watching expeditions are one of the many adventures that attract tourists to Canada.

A Man with Two Countries

One of the world's leading industrialists of the twentieth century, Cyrus S. Eaton was born in the small town of Pugwash, Nova Scotia, in 1883. As a young man, he went to the United States and became involved in the steel industry, utilities, and railroads. In 1930, he founded the Republic Steel Corporation. He made a large fortune and gave much of it to charities. During the last decades of his life he spent much of his time and energy promoting international understanding and nuclear disarmament. He founded an annual meeting in his hometown called the Pugwash Conference. Each year, key people in the sciences and education meet at his former lodge in Nova Scotia to promote international goodwill.

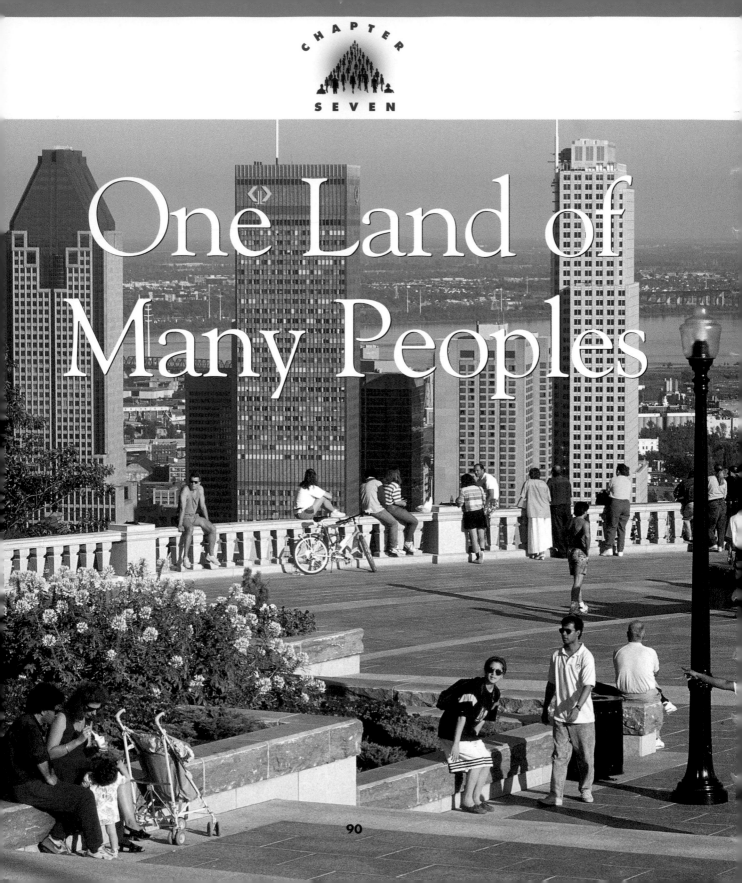

One Land of Many Peoples

CANADA'S CITIZENS COME FROM all over the world. The ancestors of many Canadians were already living here when the first Europeans arrived. They are usually called First Nations Peoples, or First Peoples, in Canada. Most of their descendants live in the northern areas of Canada. In Quebec, most people are of French ancestry, descended from early settlers and fur traders. There are also many English, Scottish, and Irish people whose ancestors arrived after the British defeated the French. More recently, Canadians have come from other parts of Europe and from Asia.

Canadians have a variety of ethnic backgrounds.

Opposite: **Canadians and foreign tourists gather on the Mont Royal Belvedere Terrace for its beautiful view of Montreal.**

A Canadian farmer and his son on their farm in Saskatchewan

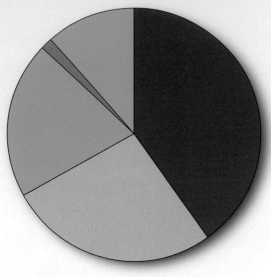

Who Lives in Canada?

■	British	40%
■	French	27%
■	Other Europeans	20%
■	First Nations Peoples	1.5%
■	Other (mostly Asians)	11.5%

In northern Quebec, on the east side of the great Hudson and James Bays, live members of the Cree nation called the Eeyou. More than 10,000 Eeyou live in nine villages and settlements in lands just below the Arctic, called the subarctic. The Eeyou hunt caribou, sea mammals, and birds for food. Most of them live near the many big rivers that flow through their land into James Bay. A few Inuit people also live in this area.

When a huge dam was built across the La Grande River to provide electricity, many Eeyou had to move from their traditional homesites. Recently, the government has made plans to build more dams on many

Members of the Cree nation congregate under a tent for a celebratory meal.

Persons per square mile	**Persons per square kilometer**
more than 260	more than 100
131–260	51–100
26–130	11–50
3–25	1–10
fewer than 3	fewer than 10

Population distribution in Canada

more rivers, and the Eeyou have banded together to protest. They say that the new dams will hurt the environment and destroy their way of life.

In addition to making changes in the way Canada is governed, the Constitution Act of 1982 recognized the rights of three main groups of aboriginal people. The First Nations are the people who lived in the lands close to the major southern rivers and lake systems and in the tundra and forests of the north. The Inuit, once called Eskimos, are the peoples who inhabited the colder regions of the tundra and snow-covered lands of the north. The Métis are people whose ancestors were the children of First Nations women who married European fur trappers and traders.

What's in a Name?

The people who inhabited Canada before Europeans came called themselves by many names, depending on what nation or tribe they belonged to, and where they lived. The first Europeans, like the early settlers in the thirteen colonies that became the United States, referred to all these original inhabitants as *Indians*.

In the past few decades, various groups in both Canada and the United States have searched for more accurate terms that would include all these aboriginal peoples. In the United States, the term *Native American* is now generally used. But in Canada, no single term is used for all these people.

Many colleges and universities have decided on *First Nations Peoples*, but not everyone agrees. Many local tribal groups do not want someone in Ottawa or Toronto telling them what their name should be. On some tribal lands, where residents have businesses and programs that teach visitors about their way of life, they do not want to change their business names and tourist brochures to keep up with what some call the "term of the week."

Some provincial governments have met with tribal leaders to find terms that different groups agree on. In New Brunswick, for example, the province has officially adopted the term *Aboriginals* to refer to Micmac and other original peoples who live there.

Throughout this book, we have most often used the term *First Nations Peoples*, but to avoid repetition and to represent varying preferences, we have also used other terms. As you read more about Canada, you will see the many names that have been used, including *Indians*.

The First Nations Peoples have representatives who deal directly with the various public bodies that affect their lives. In seeking a fair recognition of their rights and their special status in Canadian society, there have been frustrations and misunderstandings. But there have also been triumphs.

A New Name on the Map

On April 1, 1999, Canada grew larger. Its total square mileage did not increase, but it added a new territory—Nunavut. This new territory was previously part of the giant Northwest Territories. For many years, separating it had been the dream of the 27,200 residents of Nunavut's twenty-eight widely scattered communities, 85 percent of whom are Inuit.

The new territory governs itself through a nineteen-member legislature led by a premier. Its government will be based in the capital city of Iqaluit, which has a population of only 4,500.

Part of the new territory of Nunavut on Baffin Island, including the Inuit village of Kimmirut

Although their new status as an Inuit territory is a big step forward in governing themselves, it will not solve the many serious problems these communities face. People in Nunavut are desperately poor, and the prices of goods that are shipped in are very high. Nearly one-third of the people are unemployed.

Major steps toward Nunavut began in 1993, when Parliament passed an agreement giving the Inuit rights to

The Inuit

Inuit groups are named for the places where they live, such as the Mackenzie Delta, the Copper, the Netsilik, the Igulik, and the Baffinland Inuit. The groups speak somewhat different dialects, or variations, of their language—called *Inuktitut*—and have slightly different traditions. But they share a basic language and many ways of hunting.

35,000 square miles (90,643 sq km) of land that is thought to be very rich in oil and metal ores. The first job of the new government will be to find ways to extract those minerals from the ground and ship them many miles to markets around the world.

But being cut off from the rest of Canada has not been all bad. The Inuit have kept many of their old customs and preserved their culture much better than First Peoples who live in other parts of Canada. Many people still speak Inuktitut, the Inuit language.

A useful word in Inuktitut is *ayurnamat*, which translates as "That's the way it is and there's nothing we can do about it. Next time will be better." That single word says a lot about the philosophy the Inuit have about their new land.

An Inuit man standing in front of a traditional sealskin tent

People of the Cities and Coasts

Although people of Irish and Scottish backgrounds are found all over Canada, they are especially concentrated in the Atlantic provinces. Newfoundland has a high percentage of Irish, and Nova Scotia (which means New Scotland) has a large Scottish population.

Nova Scotia and New Brunswick have many Acadians—French families who have lived there since the earliest settlements. Most of them live in concentrated areas, such as the northwest coast of Nova Scotia and the northeast coast of New Brunswick. These families often fly a red, white, and blue flag with a single star, called the *Stella Maris* (star of the sea). The flag indicates their pride in their French heritage, but generally does not imply support for the French separatist movement in Quebec.

There is a large Scottish population in Nova Scotia.

An Acadian settlement in New Brunswick

Population of Major Cities

Toronto	4,263,757
Montreal	3,326,510
Vancouver	1,831,665
Ottawa	1,010,498
Edmonton	862,597
Calgary	821,628

One Land of Many Peoples **97**

Shoppers of varied ethnic backgrounds

Toronto's Chinatown

People of African descent living in Canada came from several sources. Although Toronto and Vancouver have black populations, Nova Scotia has the highest percentage. Some were brought to North America during colonial times as slaves. Others escaped slavery in the southern United States before the Civil War, making their way to safety in Canada through a network of antislavery activists known as the Underground Railroad. A large number of black people were brought to Canada by British ships that captured slave ships bound for the Caribbean and the southern United States. The ships were then sailed to Nova Scotia, where the British freed the Africans, most of whom stayed. More recently, immigrants have come to Canada directly from African nations.

Toronto has the second-largest Chinatown in North America, after San Francisco's. Vancouver also has a large Asian population. Some of these are Chinese people whose ancestors came to help build the railroad that linked Canada in the late 1800s. But from 1923 until after World War II, Canada's tight immigration policies allowed only people from European countries to enter. Almost no Chinese were allowed into Canada.

In 1962, Canada changed its policy to one of equal opportunity for all immigrants. Recently, Vancouver and Toronto have been favorites among wealthy families from Hong Kong who wanted to leave before the government of China took over control of it in 1997. Japanese people moving to Vancouver have established Canada's largest Japanese neighborhood there, with many blocks of shops, homes, markets, and other businesses owned by Japanese people. Toronto and Vancouver have the largest percentages of Asian Canadians.

A Japanese garden in Victoria, British Columbia

Many Peoples, Many Faiths

SAINT PETER'S

102

CANADIANS ARE FREE TO WORSHIP AS THEY CHOOSE— or not to worship at all. All the world's major religions have followers in Canada. The spiritual and religious beliefs of most Canadians are based on those of their ancestors. French and Irish settlers and later immigrants brought Roman Catholicism with them, while British settlers brought a variety of Protestant faiths. Recent immigrants have expanded Canada's Muslim population and brought other religions from Asia, such as Buddhism

Opposite: **Saint Peter's Catholic church in Nova Scotia**

Saint Paul's Anglican Church in Trinity, Newfoundland

The ornate interior of the Notre Dame Basilica in Montreal

The Catholic Church in Canadian Life

In the mostly French province of Quebec, the Roman Catholic Church is a very strong influence, playing a major role in everyday life. But not all Canada's Catholics are French people living in Quebec. New Brunswick, Nova Scotia, and Prince Edward Island also have large French Catholic populations, as well as Catholics of Irish descent. Newfoundland is heavily Irish, and most of those residents are practicing Catholics too. Toronto has a large population of Italian Catholics. In all, 46 percent—nearly half—of Canadians are Catholics.

For French Canadians in Quebec—especially in the smaller towns, where social and community life is still closely tied to the Church—Christmas is an important religious holiday, as well as an occasion for exchanging gifts. The

Marguerite Bourgeoys

Very little is known about the early life of Marguerite Bourgeoys in France, but she came to Montreal with the first French settlers, living in the fort and caring for the settlers and soldiers. In 1658, she opened a school for women—the first in New France—and trained all its teachers. She founded the religious order of Sisters of the Congregation of Notre Dame. When she died in 1700, nearly everyone in Montreal came to her funeral. In 1982, she was canonized (made a saint) by the Catholic Church.

celebration begins with midnight Mass on December 24. After returning home through the cold night, people enjoy a big meal called a *réveillon*. This usually includes hearty stews and other traditional dishes, such as a meat pie called *tourtière*.

Religious Traditions

Most Protestants in Canada belong to the United Church of Canada or churches of the Anglican Communion. The United Church was established in Toronto in 1925, uniting most Congregational, Methodist, and Presbyterian churches in Canada. Anglican churches follow the traditions of the Church of England.

For many Canadians whose families immigrated from other countries, their church is a way of keeping their culture alive. Ukrainians, for example, celebrate Easter—a major holiday in the Ukraine—with church services and activities that follow the traditional Eastern Orthodox religion and customs. They decorate Easter eggs with delicate designs, using beeswax to form fine lines before dipping the eggs in richly colored dyes. These eggs symbolize the resurrection of Christ.

Ukrainian children decorating traditional Easter eggs at their home in Saskatchewan

First Nations Peoples

Most traditional spiritual holidays of the First Nations Peoples follow the natural seasons, celebrating the arrival of spring, or the winter equinox, when days begin to get longer. Many traditional beliefs are expressed in stories that have been passed down from parents to children for generations. These stories often explain the universe—how rivers and lakes were formed, why the sun rises and sets, and why animals behave as they do. In the Haida and many other cultures, these stories also show how people should behave toward one another and toward nature. In this way, they build and maintain moral and social values while keeping people in touch with their spiritual traditions.

Many Haida stories tell of the consequences of not respecting nature. They remind the Haida how much their lives depend on their treatment of the natural world. One story tells of two boys who deliberately break the wings of a duck just to be mean and are turned into killer whales. Another tells of a man who throws a live frog into the fire: A volcano suddenly erupts and destroys his village and everyone in it except two people who had tried to rescue the frog. The messages of these and other stories are very clear: Be kind to nature and nature will be kind to you; hurt nature and it will strike back.

When loggers tried to cut down the old forests of the islands where one group of Haida lived, the Haida protested. They tried to stop the destruction, not only because this was their home, but because they had always been taught to respect nature. These beliefs do not conflict with the faith of organized

religions, and many Haida practice both—attending church regularly and taking part in traditional ceremonies too.

The Igloo Church in Inuvik

Many of these original Canadians also belong to other churches. In some communities, their Christian churches are built in shapes that represent the local cultures. In Inuvik, the Catholic church is shaped like an igloo, and the church in Fort Franklin, Northwest Territories, has a roof shaped like a teepee.

Canada has no official religion, and although prayers are often said at public meetings and on ceremonial occasions, no organized religion influences the Canadian government. But the government does support some religious institutions with money. Organizations that provide health and social services, as well as schools run by churches, can get federal aid.

Canadian Culture

Costumed dancers
entertaining a crowd at the
Confederation of the Arts

Canada's healthy and supportive cultural climate encourages artists, writers, filmmakers, musicians, and actors. Large cities and small towns have regular arts events that involve local performers and encourage schoolchildren to participate in music and dance. Several major cities have their own opera or ballet companies and symphony orchestras; the Royal Winnipeg Ballet (in Manitoba) and the Montreal Symphony Orchestra are among the most important.

Opposite: **Kayaking is a popular outdoor activity.**

Bagpipes to Shakespeare

Canadians love festivals, which bring together well-known artists in large events that are attended by thousands of people. One of the best known is the Stratford Shakespeare Festival in Stratford, west of Toronto. Although most famous for its Shakespearean stage, Stratford is also the home of several other excellent theaters. The annual Shaw Festival, in Niagara-on-the-Lake, near Niagara Falls, performs the work of the British playwright George Bernard Shaw each summer.

The Miramichi region of New Brunswick, on the East Coast, has the largest summer festival of Irish music and dance outside of Ireland, with musicians and storytellers from all over the world. On Cape Breton Island, Nova Scotia, Celtic Colours International Festival is celebrated for two weeks each fall, bringing Scottish singers, pipers, and other musicians to perform in towns and villages all over the island. All summer, the Gaelic College in Saint Anne, also on Cape Breton Island, has regular Scottish and Irish music and art events. Weekly *ceilidhs* (KAY-lees) and square dances are all part of everyday life in several towns.

Bagpipers in Nova Scotia

Throughout Atlantic Canada, many people of Irish or Scottish origin, especially the Scottish, maintain strong ties with their culture. This is most apparent in the musical traditions, and this heritage, combined with the strong traditions of fishing and other maritime trades, has created a special kind of music, called maritime music. It is a blend of seafaring songs with the sounds of Irish ballads and Scottish airs. Especially in Halifax and St. John's, Newfoundland, the sounds of maritime music are commonly heard in clubs and at concerts.

Canadian pop sensation Celine Dion

Each region of Canada offers a distinct climate for artists, reflecting the history and background of the people. Quebec is especially rich in Francophone (French-speaking) culture, and almost any night in Montreal you can find plays, musical shows, poetry readings, or other performances in French. In rural areas of Quebec province, lively concerts of country fiddle music, usually accompanied by dancing and singing, are held nearly every weekend.

Some Canadian pop and rock stars are Celine Dion, Alanis Morisette, Shania Twain, and Sarah McLachlan. Spirit of the West is a popular singing group, while Capercaillie and the Irish Descendents are known throughout Canada and the United States for their Celtic music. Natalie MacMasters is a popular Celtic singer.

Many Canadian writers have found inspiration for their work in their country's rich history. Farley Mowat is one of Canada's best-known and best-loved authors. Mowat writes about many subjects, and several of his books are based on historical periods. *The Desperate People*, for instance, tells about the plight of a native tribe threatened by civilization. Pierre Berton is just as famous for his historical writing. In addition to his historical nonfiction (*The Last Spike* and *Flames across the Border*), he has written a large series of historical fiction for younger readers.

Contemporary writer Margaret Atwood holding her novel *Alias Grace*

Prince Edward Island writer Lucy Maud Montgomery wrote a series of books for young people about her childhood and youth on the island. Still well-known and loved, *Anne of Green Gables*—the first of these books, published in 1909—was made into a popular movie. Each summer, her island home celebrates Montgomery's work with performances of *Anne of Green Gables* at the Charlottetown Festival.

Margaret Atwood is a popular contemporary writer whose novel *The Handmaid's Tale* was made into a movie. Timothy Findley's *The Wars* and his humorous *Not Wanted on the*

Where Book Characters Come to Life

In much the same way as the characters and places in *Anne of Green Gables* have become a symbol of Prince Edward Island, the fictional characters and places in Antonine Maillet's books have become a symbol of New Brunswick's Acadian French population. Le Pays de la Sagouine is an Acadian stage set, built just as the town is described in Maillet's books. Located on an island, it is a make-believe town of song, dance, fiddle music, Acadian food, traditional crafts, history, and storytelling—all bringing Maillet's characters to life.

Voyage are popular in Canada and elsewhere, as are books by Margaret Laurence (*The Stone Angel*), Robertson Davies (*The Deptford Trilogy*), and W.O. Mitchell. Joy Kogawa writes about Japanese Canadians, and Paul Yee writes children's stories, especially about Chinese Canadians. The successful movie *Field of Dreams* was based on the W. P. Kinsella book *Shoeless Joe*. In 1994, Carol Shields won the Pulitzer Prize for *The Stone Diaries*. James Houston writes adventure stories about the North for children and adults.

With so much wilderness and such a variety of interesting animals, it is not surprising that Canada has so many writers who use nature as their theme. The movie *Never Cry Wolf* was based on Farley Mowat's book *Endangered Spaces* and looks closely at the importance of the wilderness to Canadians. Montreal nature writer Fred Bruemmer has written a number of books on seals, polar bears, and other animals of the Far North.

A Rich Legacy of Art

Canada's vast and beautiful natural world also inspired many of its artists and even led them to become recognized as a separate

Canada's Largest Museum

The Royal Ontario Museum in Toronto has something for everyone. An entire Chinese tomb, Egyptian mummy cases, priceless gems, Roman sculptures, and dinosaurs fill its collections. It even has a bat cave.

art movement. Breaking away from the traditional—almost photographic—painting techniques and styles of the past, several Canadian artists began to paint their native landscapes in a new way, using vivid colors and bold strokes to hint at reality instead of reproducing it exactly, as earlier artists had done.

In the early 1900s, this was quite a revolutionary idea in conservative Canada, and at first Canadian art critics disapproved. But as European critics began to praise this work, people at home took another look. They soon were very proud of the artists they called the Group of Seven. Many of the works of these seven painters, often known as the "fathers of Canadian impressionism," are exhibited in the Art Gallery of Ontario, an outstanding art museum in Toronto.

A painting by Arthur Lismer, an original member of the Group of Seven

An Inuit carving made of soapstone

Although the work of Inuit carvers and other artists was appreciated as an ethnic craft and admired by local collectors, it took a long time for their work to be recognized as a fine art form of its own. Today, Inuit art is highly prized by museums, galleries, and collectors. Artists such as Davidialiek Amiituk, an eastern Inuit who works in both printmaking and carving, and painter/carver Mingo Martin, who created the world's tallest totem pole for a park in Victoria, British Columbia, have brought worldwide recognition to their people's cultural themes and designs.

Canadians on Film

Many Canadian actors have become popular in Hollywood movies. Some of the better-

Atlantic Coast Artists

David Blackwood and Thomas Forrestall both draw their inspiration from the rugged Atlantic coast of their native provinces. Forrestall, who is Nova Scotia's best-known artist, paints coastal landscapes.

Blackwood, who was born in Newfoundland, takes a more historical view of the seaport towns and their ships and people, using them as the themes for his highly prized etchings.

known stars are Michael J. Fox, Margot Kidder, Jim Carrey, Leslie Nielsen, and the late John Candy. Feature films by Canadian filmmakers include *Jesus of Montreal* by Denys Arcand, *The Fly* by David Cronenberg, *The Sweet Hereafter* by Atom Egoyen, and *Titanic* by James Cameron.

Popular actor Jim Carrey is originally from Canada.

Hockey Is King

Canadians, whether they come from very British Victoria or fiercely French Montreal, can all agree on at least one thing: Hockey is the world's most exciting, interesting, and important sport. They not only like to watch their favorite

Children all over Canada love to play ice hockey.

Two Hockey Greats

Wayne Gretzky (left) was born in Ontario, the youngest athlete ever to play in the major leagues of any sport. He led his team, the Edmonton Oilers, to win three Stanley Cups and broke nearly every record in hockey, including two records for the number of points scored in a season, the second time with 215 points.

One of the longest active careers of any professional athlete was that of Gordie Howe (right), who played thirty-two seasons, most of them with the Detroit Red Wings. In those thirty-two years, this Saskatchewan native scored more than 1,000 goals and 1,500 assists

teams play hockey, they like to play it themselves, on ice in the winter and on pavement courts the rest of the year.

Six National Hockey League teams represent Canada's largest cities. They are the Toronto Maple Leafs, the Montreal Canadiens, the Ottawa Senators, the Vancouver Canucks, the Calgary Flames, and the Edmonton Oilers.

Canada has its own football league, with teams representing Toronto, Edmonton, Hamilton, Montreal, Winnipeg, Calgary, British Columbia, and Saskatchewan. Canada's two

largest cities have baseball teams, both franchises of U.S. leagues. The Toronto Blue Jays are in the American League, and the Montreal Expos are in the National League. The Blue Jays have won the World Series twice.

Although basketball is not as popular as hockey, football, and baseball, Canada has professional basketball teams. Since 1996, the Toronto Raptors and the Vancouver Grizzlies have been members of the NBA.

It is not surprising that Canadians excel at ice skating, or that they have done very well in recent World Figure Skating Championships. Elvis Stojko won the title in 1994, 1995, and 1997. Kurt Browning won from 1989 through 1991

Whistler ski resort

and again in 1993, and Brian Orser won the title in 1987. Canadians have also won Olympic medals in the individual sports of skiing, swimming, track, and speed-skating.

Individual sports are popular with Canadians, especially those activities that take place outdoors. Skiing is a major winter sport, and no wonder, since Canada has some of the finest ski resorts in the world. From Whistler, in British Columbia, to Mont Tremblant in Quebec's Laurentian Mountains, Canada's ski slopes attract international skiers as well as Canadians. Along with skiing, people take to the snow on toboggans, sleds, snowshoes, snowmobiles, and dogsleds.

Sports are an important school activity, and Canadian children are encouraged to learn and take part in as many as they can. Even many small communities have public sports complexes with indoor skating rinks, ball courts, and swimming pools. Schools use them for regular swimming programs, teams practice and train in them, and they are open to the public for recreation. In Montreal, the giant stadium built for the swimming competitions in the 1976 Olympics is now a public sports facility. Schoolchildren learn to swim in the same pool where Olympic gold medals were won.

Sampling Outdoor Sports

Outdoor activities are so much a part of life in New Brunswick that the province has found a way to share these activities with others. The Day Adventure program encourages visitors and local people alike to choose from a "catalog" of day and half-day activities, complete with equipment and instruction. Adults and young people who have never paddled a kayak or canoe, climbed rocks on a rope, explored a cave, sailed a boat, ridden a horse, mushed a dogsled team, or slid down a hill on skis can learn the basics and enjoy trying their new skills in New Brunswick's great outdoors.

Living in Canada

T HE DAILY LIVES OF CANADA'S MANY PEOPLES ARE THE best examples of the nation's great diversity. Let's meet a few of these people.

Paul Arlookto, an Inuit child in the new territory of Nunavut, is walking home from school in the dark. He left home in the morning under a black sky too, hardly seeing daylight at all in the short winter days near the North Pole. Luckily, he doesn't have to walk far in the icy Arctic wind to reach his warm one-story house. The town he lives in, Nunavut's capital of Iqaluit, is very small; only 4,500 people live there.

Opposite: **Teepees on a Blackfoot reservation in Alberta**

Inuit children making music in their spare time

In Newfoundland, Brian Cleary, the son of a fisher on Cape Saint Mary's, is hard at work helping his father mend nets that were torn in last week's storm. As he watches his father hurry to fix them so he won't miss another day's catch, Brian wonders if there will be enough fish left in the sea for him to follow his father's way of life. In the evening, before they all fall into bed, he may listen to his mother sing a few haunting songs of her parents' Irish homeland.

Children rowing a boat in the harbor of a fishing village on a summer evening

National Holidays in Canada

New Year's Day	January 1
Good Friday	March–April (varies)
Easter Sunday	March–April (varies)
Victoria Day	Monday nearest May 24
Canada Day	July 1
Labour Day	First Monday in September
Thanksgiving Day	Second Monday in October
Christmas Day	December 25
Boxing Day	December 26

A Canada Day crowd in Ottawa

Elementary school students learning English as a second language in Vancouver

In Vancouver, far to the west, Kumi Tanaka leaves her public school at 2:20 P.M. and hurries to begin her second school day. She catches a bus to join other children at a Japanese school, where she polishes her skills in reading in the language of her ancestors. After reading, she will write, using a brush and ink to form the intricate characters that take the place of letters. In the evening, she must complete homework assignments from both schools before she unfolds her futon and goes to bed.

In Nobleton, a suburb north of Toronto, Nancy Norton hurries to her art

Living in Canada   **123**

Homes in the residential neighborhood of Cabbagetown, Toronto

teacher's house after school, hoping that she will have the news Nancy has been waiting for. Nancy can hardly wait to find out how her painting of the sunset over Lake Ontario fared with the judges in the art contest. As she walks, Nancy dreams of someday being a well-known painter and having her work hang with Canada's great "Northern Light" painters in the nearby McMichael Canadian Art Collection.

Some Canadian Foods

Most Canadians eat just about the same foods as everyone else in Canada and the United States, but each region has its local favorites. Dulce is a snack made of dried seaweed, which people in the Atlantic provinces gather on the shore. New Brunswick is known as the "Fiddlehead Capital of the World" because of the tender, tasty vegetables gathered there early each spring. Fiddleheads (below) are the tightly curled new shoots of a special kind of fern. Bakeapples are really not apples at all, but small orange berries with a slightly smoky flavor. These are a particular treat in Newfoundland, but they grow in bogs and low areas across the Far North, too. British Columbia is known for its variety of wild woodland berries, such as the juicy purple boysenberry. These are served fresh in the summer and made into jams and jellies or frozen so that people can enjoy their sweet flavor all year round.

Children of Scottish descent dancing at a festival in Antigonish, Nova Scotia

In Antigonish, on the northern shore of Nova Scotia, Annie MacGregor is stitching the hem of her kilt, torn on the way home from last Sunday night's *ceilidh*, where she and her friends danced until they were exhausted. She needs to have her kilt fixed and pressed by Saturday, when she will march in a parade with her fellow bagpipers. Her band will also march at the annual Highland Games in the summer. Visitors fill her town that week to watch competitions of bagpipe bands, Scottish dancing, and sports. Annie's older brother is competing for the first time this year in the caber toss.

Yvette Marceau, in the Quebec town of Manouane, is helping her mother grind pork for *tourtière*, and her mouth is already watering at the thought of it. But the meat has to simmer for hours with spices before it is mixed with mashed potatoes and put between two flaky tender crusts to bake in the oven. The wait seems like days, as its wonderful aroma fills the house. The savory pie will be tomorrow morning's breakfast, hearty enough to keep her father working in the woods all morning. But Yvette doesn't mind waiting for breakfast, since dinner is on the back of the big black woodstove—a pot of rich green-pea soup with chunks of ham floating in it.

It's just another typical day in Canada.

A girl talking to a vendor on the streets of Montreal

The Man Who Changed Life in the Far North

J. Armand Bombardier (1907–1964) was an inventor from Quebec. His most famous invention is the snowmobile, which travels over snow as easily a car travels on a road. Not only did he create a sport enjoyed by hundreds of thousands of people, but he made it possible for people to travel across much of Canada in the winter, changing life forever in the remote communities of the North. His family's company still manufactures snowmobiles.

Timeline

Canadian History

First people cross a land bridge from Asia to North America.	8000 B.C.
Dorset culture develops in eastern Arctic Canada.	800 B.C.— A.D. 1200
Eric the Red, a Viking, explores Baffin Island.	982
Leif Eriksson, or other Vikings, form a colony at L'Anse aux Meadows, Newfoundland.	1000
The Dorset Culture has been replaced by the Thule peoples.	1200
John Cabot explores Newfoundland and Canada's eastern shore.	1497
Jacques Cartier explores the Gulf of St. Lawrence, followed by Samuel de Champlain; France claims the new lands.	1535
Newfoundland and its fisheries are claimed for England by Humphrey Gilbert.	1583
Hudson's Bay Company is founded.	1670
Hudson Bay, Newfoundland, and much of Eastern Canada are ceded to Britain by France in the Treaty of Utrecht.	1713
Acadians are expelled from Nova Scotia, Prince Edward Island, and New Brunswick.	1755
The British defeat the French at Quebec; Montreal is taken by the English.	1759–1760
France gives up its colony in Canada.	1763

World History

2500 B.C.	Egyptians build the Pyramids and Sphinx in Giza.
563 B.C.	Buddha is born in India.
A.D. 313	The Roman emperor Constantine recognizes Christianity.
610	The prophet Muhammad begins preaching a new religion called Islam.
1054	The Eastern (Orthodox) and Western (Roman) Churches break apart.
1066	William the Conqueror defeats the English in the Battle of Hastings.
1095	Pope Urban II proclaims the First Crusade.
1215	King John seals the Magna Carta.
1300s	The Renaissance begins in Italy.
1347	The Black Death sweeps through Europe.
1453	Ottoman Turks capture Constantinople, conquering the Byzantine Empire.
1492	Columbus arrives in North America.
1500s	The Reformation leads to the birth of Protestantism.

Canadian History

Britain's Parliament gives French Canadians political and religious freedoms.	1774
Britain fights the United States in the War of 1812; many battles are fought along the Canadian border.	1812–1815
A rebellion breaks out in Quebec and Ontario provinces.	1837
Quebec and Ontario join to become the Province of Canada with their own Parliament.	1848
Nova Scotia, New Brunswick, Quebec, and Ontario form a confederation called the Dominion of Canada.	1867
Canada buys the lands of the North and West from the Hudson's Bay Company.	1869
Manitoba, British Columbia, and Prince Edward Island join the confederation; Northwest Territories is established.	1870–1873
The Canadian Pacific Railroad links Canada from coast to coast; Métis revolt in Saskatchewan is put down.	1885
Gold is discovered in Yukon; Yukon is organized as Yukon Territory.	1896–1898
Saskatchewan and Alberta join the Confederation.	1905
Canadian troops fight for Britain in World War I.	1914–1918
Complete independence is granted by the Statute of Westminster.	1931
Canada fights World War II in Europe and the Pacific; Canadian ports serve convoys.	1939–1945
Newfoundland joins the confederation.	1949
The Saint Lawrence Seaway opens.	1959
A referendum calling for Quebec independence is defeated.	1980
A second independence referendum is defeated narrowly.	1998
Nunavut Territory is formed.	1999

World History

1776	The Declaration of Independence is signed.
1789	The French Revolution begins.
1865	The American Civil War ends.
1914	World War I breaks out.
1917	The Bolshevik Revolution brings Communism to Russia.
1929	Worldwide economic depression begins.
1939	World War II begins, following the German invasion of Poland.
1957	The Vietnam War starts.
1989	The Berlin Wall is torn down, as Communism crumbles in Eastern Europe.
1996	Bill Clinton is reelected U.S. president.

Fast Facts

Official name: Canada

Capital: Ottawa

Official languages: English and French

A Haida mask

Canadian flag

Banff National Park

Official religion:	None
Year of founding:	July 1, 1867
National anthem:	"O Canada"
Type of government:	Confederation with a parliamentary democracy
Chief of state:	British monarch, through a governor-general
Head of government:	Prime minister
Area:	3,851,809 square miles (9,976,185 sq km)
Bordering country:	United States of America
Highest elevation:	Mount Logan, 19,524 feet (5,951 m), in the Yukon Territory
Lowest elevation:	Sea level
Average temperature extremes:	–26°F (–33°C) Arctic Bay, Northwest Territories; 70°F (21°C) Ottawa, Ontario
Average annual precipitation:	0.5 inch (1.3 cm) a month in Arctic Bay, Northwest Territories; 4.8 inches (12.2 cm) a month in Vancouver, British Columbia
National population (1999 est.):	31,006,347

Population of major cities (greater metropolitan area):

Toronto	4,263,757
Montreal	3,326,510
Vancouver	1,831,665
Ottawa/Hull	1,010,498
Edmonton	862,597
Calgary	821,628

Rocks on the Bay of Fundy

Famous landmarks: Many of Canada's most famous places are its natural and scenic wonders, such as Niagara Falls (which it shares with the United States), Banff and Lake Louise, Fundy National Park, and the Cabot Trail on Cape Breton Island. Historic landmarks include the reconstructed Fortress of Louisbourg in Nova Scotia and The Citadels in Quebec and Halifax. The CN Tower dominates the skyline of Toronto as the tallest structure in Canada, and the striking modern buildings built as pavilions for the Expos, or world's fairs, in Montreal and Vancouver are landmarks on the shores of each city.

Industry: Canada's chief agricultural products are wheat, barley, and corn. The most important minerals mined or extracted are crude petroleum, copper, and zinc. The chief manufactured products are cars and trucks, paper and wood products, and telecommunications equipment.

Currency: The unit of currency is the Canadian dollar. In early 2000, U.S.$1 = 1.4496 Canadian dollars.

Currency

System of weights and measures: Metric system

Literacy rate: 97%

Common Canadian words and phrases:

Acadian	A French resident of one of the Atlantic provinces
Bergy bits	A Newfoundland term for the pieces that break off icebergs as they float into warmer waters
Ceilidh	A party with Celtic (Scottish and Irish) music and dancing
Coureurs de bois	Early French fur traders
Habitants	Original French settlers who remained when the British took over New France

Canadian schoolchildren

Wayne Gretzky

Loonie	Popular term for the $1 coin, which pictures a loon
Mounties	The Royal Canadian Mounted Police
Northwest Passage	A route connecting the Saint Lawrence River to the Pacific Ocean by water; early explorers searched for it unsuccessfully
Québécois	French people of Quebec Province
Quebecer	Any resident of Quebec Province
The Rock	Newfoundlanders' pet name for their island province
Sugar shack	A place in the countryside of Quebec province where maple sugar is made and people gather for traditional French Canadian food, music, and dancing
Toonie	Popular name for Canada's $2 coin
Voyageur	A large canoe that carried groups of traders and supplies

Famous people:

J. Armand Bombardier (1907–1964)
Inventor

Saint Marguerite Bourgeoys (1620–1700)
Educator

Samuel de Champlain (1567–1635)
French explorer

Wayne Gretzky (1961–)
Hockey player

Sir John Macdonald (1815–1891)
First prime minister of the Dominion of Canada

Alexander Mackenzie (1764–1820)
European explorer

Paul Okalik (1965–)
Premier of Nunavut

Pierre Elliott Trudeau (1919–)
Prime minister

To Find Out More

Nonfiction

▶ Brown, Craig. *Illustrated History of Canada*. Toronto: Key Porter Books, 1997.

▶ Grabowski, John F. *Canada*. Modern Nations of the World. San Diego: Lucent Books, 1998.

▶ LeVert, Suzanne. *Canada Facts & Figures*. Let's Discover Canada. New York: Chelsea House, 1992.

▶ LeVert, Suzanne. *Dominion of Canada*. Let's Discover Canada. New York: Chelsea House, 1992.

▶ LeVert, Suzanne. Let's Discover Canada. [Series.] New York: Chelsea House, 1992. *This series includes a book for each province in addition to the two titles cited above.*

▶ National Geographic Society. *Traveling the Trans-Canada*. Washington, D.C.: National Geographic Society, 1987.

▶ Siy, Alexandra. *The Eeyou: People of Eastern James Bay*. New York: Dillon Press, 1993.

Websites

▶ **Government of Canada**
http://canada.gc.ca/main_e.html
The official website of the government of Canada displays a wealth of information about all the territories and provinces, including maps, contact information, and links to the official government sites of each territory.

▶ **Gateway to Nunavut**
http://www.nunavut.com/
The official website of the territory of Nunavut; includes basic facts, the Nunavut Handbook, *the* Nunatsiaq News *(partly in Inuktitut), a Nunavut business directory, contact information, maps, and the magazine* Nunavut '99: Changing the Map of Canada.

▶ Nova Scotia

http://www.gov.ns.ca/

The official website of Nova Scotia;
includes information on government,
travel and tourism, business and
investing, current and past news
releases, and basic facts.

▶ Quebec

http://www.gouv.qc.ca/introa.htm

The official website of the government
of Quebec in English, Spanish, and
French; includes information on the
territory, society, health, education,
culture, businesses, and current news.

▶ Wilderness Committee

http://www.wildernesscommittee.org/
endangered_species.htm

The official website of the Western
Canada Wilderness Committee
(WCWC); includes information on
endangered species, ancient forests,
current and past news, contacts,
and membership.

Embassies and Organizations

▶ **Embassy of Canada**
501 Pennsylvania Avenue, NW
Washington, DC 20001
(202) 682-1740
http://www.canadianembassy.org/

▶ **Canadian Consulate General**
Two Prudential Plaza
180 N. Stetson Avenue, Suite 2400
Chicago, IL 60601
(312) 616-1860
http://www.canadaonlinechicago.net/

▶ **Canadian Consulate General**
1251 Avenue of the Americas
New York, NY 10020
(212) 596-1628
http://www.canada-ny.org/

▶ **Canadian Consulate General**
750 N. St. Paul Street, Suite 1700
Dallas, TX 75201
www.canada-dallas.org/

Index

Page numbers in *italics* indicate illustrations.

Meet the Authors

BARBARA AND STILLMAN ROGERS TRAVELED TO CANADA each summer with their children for many years before they began writing about it. They have written several guidebooks to eastern Canada including, most recently, *Adventure Guide to Canada's Atlantic Provinces*. In researching that book, they traveled through every part of the four eastern provinces, hiking, kayaking, and even dogsledding. They have already begun research for a similar book on the province of Quebec. Stillman is the author of *Montreal* in the Cities of the World series, published by Children's Press.

Along with Canadian subjects, the Rogerses have written books on New England, where they live, and Europe and Africa, where they have traveled frequently. They are the authors of books on South Africa, Zambia, and Peru. Barbara

and their daughter Lura, who has traveled with them since she was a child, are coauthors of *Dominican Republic* in the Enchantment of the World Series.

While researching this book on Canada, they traveled from Vancouver Island to Newfoundland, stayed with local families, and even spent a night in an igloo built of snow blocks. They found the colorful, magazine-style publications of the provincial and city tourism offices to be very helpful. "Although these are designed for travelers planning their trips, the color photographs and descriptions give a vivid picture of the landscapes, the wildlife, and the way people live," the Rogerses advise, and they recommend that readers send for these free magazines to see Canada's tremendous variety.

Photo Credits